Just Listen

ALSO BY NANCY O'HARA

Find a Quiet Corner

Nancy O'Hara

Just Listen

A Guide to Finding Your Own True Voice

BROADWAY BOOKS · NEW YORK

B
BROADWAY

A hardcover edition of this book was published in 1997 by Broadway Books.

Broadway Books titles may be purchased for business or promotional use or for special sales. For information, please write to: Special Markets Department, Bantam Doubleday Dell Publishing Group, Inc., 1540 Broadway, New York, NY 10036.

BROADWAY BOOKS *and its logo, a letter B bisected on the diagonal, are trademarks of Broadway Books, a division of Bantam Doubleday Dell Publishing Group, Inc.*

First trade paperback edition published 1998.

Designed by Ellen Cipriano

The Library of Congress has catalogued the hardcover as:

O'Hara, Nancy.
   Just listen : a guide to finding your own true voice / by Nancy
O'Hara. — 1st ed.
      p.   cm.
   ISBN 0-7679-0022-7 (hardcover)
      1. Spiritual life.   2. Self-actualization (Psychology)—Religious
aspects.   3. O'Hara, Nancy.   I. Title.
   BL624.034 1997
   291.4—DC21   97-20106
                                                              CIP

ISBN 0-7679-0023-5

99 00 01 02 10 9 8 7 6 5 4 3 2

To all my teachers everywhere

known and unknown—
past, present, and future.
And most especially to Mom,
my very first teacher.

C O N T E N T S

Book II: Acceptance

Book III: Taking Action

ACKNOWLEDGMENTS

With hands together, I bow in gratitude and send thanks and love to my spiritual friends and teachers. To Eido Roshi, my teacher in so many ways, who tells me over and over again that my life is not just about me. To Sarah Jane Freymann, agent, friend, and fellow traveler who contributed her unique wisdom to help shape this book. To John Michel, editor extraordinaire, who has a gift for giving and who helped all along the way. To Lauren Marino, my editor at Broadway, whose insight and enthusiasm for this project helped guide me through it. To Bill, Bob, and Lois for their wisdom and inspiration. To Perry Klepner, who gave unconditionally and listened without judgment. To Toinette Lippe for her help with the title. To Nancy Berg and Rinaldo Petronio—my two wise guardian angels. To Ruth O'Hara Lewis, Barbara Suter, Tom Fuller, Leslie Bauman, Ruth Mendum, Sarah Baker, and Steve Regan, who graciously allowed a part of their lives to be included here to teach us all. To Deb Darrock for opening her heart and believing in me as a writer. To Tom, Jeannie, Kim, Amy, and Gina for just being there each week, listening, and letting me be me. To Dunja Lingwood, who ever reminds me to lead with my heart. To all my dharma brothers and sisters, especially those at Shobo-ji and Dai Bosatsu. To everyone at Cafe 112, especially Moustafa and Doma, who offered good food and a quiet corner for writing. And to all the folks at Broadway who have contributed something important to this book, including visionary publisher Bill Shinker, Maggie Richards, Roberto de Vicq de Cumptich, Kathy Spinelli, Trigg Robinson, Don Weisberg, and Kati Steele.

Just Listen

INTRODUCTION

When we are born we are more dependent on our mothers and for a longer period of time than any other creature. Since we cannot feed, clothe, and shelter ourselves without help, we are forced to rely on others, which is natural and necessary. As we get older, we continue to rely on others, and the circle of people we rely on gets larger. Yet many of us lose ourselves as we look to others to help us decide how we should think, feel, act, and just be in the world. Many of us shape ourselves around what others want us to be, how others expect us to act—usually unconsciously. Somewhere along the line we begin to lose touch with our own individual essence.

Although we often know what we want and how we want to get it, when our needs and desires challenge what our caretakers believe is good for us, we often deny our inner selves so we don't disappoint others. We alter ourselves to fit in, to be accepted, to be loved. For ultimately it is probably just love that we are seeking, and we'll do almost anything to get that love, including self-sacrifice. We learn to believe that what we think, want, or feel is not necessarily right, true, or good. So we conform to others' ideas of us and whom we should be, further and further sinking our unique personal truth deeper and deeper into our beings. This self-truth—our inner voice—gets covered over with years of neglect and conformity, and it moves further and further out of our reach. We then live our lives looking toward others, and not just our parents, for approval. We look toward others to satisfy our love needs, never learning how to nurture and love ourselves. We are forever and always other-dependent, even those of us (especially those of us!) who have rebelled and become what we think of as self-reliant, self-sufficient. Beneath this delusion is a desperate yearning to connect with others, to get love and approval from others, though we usually don't recognize that. And though we may feel that our lives are self-directed and that we're doing what we want, whenever we want, more than likely we yearn for that love and approval while our inner lives remain trapped in the web of self-denial and delusion.

I awakened to this denial in my own life twelve years ago, when my father died. I had gradually been shutting out the world without truly being aware of it. My life had become incredibly small, and I was using intoxicants to feel anything, even just alive. But my father's death penetrated deep into my being—I realized that my life was so empty because I was afraid to die and therefore was afraid to live. With my father's death, and for the first time in many years, I wanted to live and not simply to exist. Thus began my journey toward myself and a spiritual life. The real me was struggling to get out.

I began by recognizing that I could no longer anesthetize myself with drugs and alcohol if I were to live a full and enriching life. I sought help, and on June 10, 1985, I made a vow to myself to live a life of sobriety from that day forward. Then the real work began. Slowly I gained confidence and trusted that to build a new life I needed to begin from ground zero. In a sense I was like a newborn. Little by little, one moment at a time, I learned different ways to be in the world, ways that didn't compromise who I am at the core of my deepest and truest self. It took time, patience, pain, mistakes, and a lot more to finally learn that I am—and that each one of us is—innately perfect, and that I simply need to be authentic within myself to wake up and really experience life.

After putting down drugs and alcohol, my mind and body—

all my sensations—began to wake up. However, I wasn't prepared for the noise in my head—a constant internal dialogue that I couldn't control. My mind finally had my attention, and it wouldn't leave me alone. It would look at the past, going over and over what had happened, what hadn't happened, what should have happened, what I could have done. It would project into the future and dream about possibility or a new life; or it would worry about potential disaster. My mother's voice, my father's voice, and many other voices that I picked up and absorbed over the years would chime in now and then, trying to help me sort out my life. But rather than helping, they only added to my confusion, and nothing was clear. At first the lively dialogue was a refreshing change from the dullness that the intoxicants had perpetuated. But at times I thought the constant chatter would drive me nuts.

In 1988 I suffered a broken heart from the rejection of a cherished lover. Now a voice was telling me that I was not only unloved but unlovable. Yet through this din I heard something telling me that I needed to deepen my spiritual commitment to myself and that this would help quiet the mental noise. So in desperation I went on a retreat to a Zen Buddhist monastery to learn how to meditate. I was told that the practice of meditation would help quiet my mind. Sure enough, the noise abated, and through sitting still and meditating I realized that much of it was simply a diversion and that it was possible to sit in silence and find myself. I realized that the only thing in my way was fear. So I faced that fear and continued to meditate, quieting my mind in search of my true self, my own inner voice.

My life began to change as a result of this practice, and I began to gain a measure of peace and serenity. I thought that I was doing quite well, until November 1991, when I lost a job that I loved and another meaningful relationship. The trauma I suffered from these losses taught me that I was still clinging to things and people, which had become all too important in defining who I was. I was still looking outside myself for internal peace.

I decided to use the gift of unemployment to spend some extended time at the monastery, to further deepen my spiritual practice, to learn more about this clinging business and how to let go before things are wrenched away from me. I wanted to learn how to detach from things and people yet still love them. I wanted to go even deeper into myself to learn what I wanted from this life, what it is that moves me. And I wanted to do this without ego. So I lived on top of a mountain in a glorious, peaceful setting for five months.

When I returned to New York City and reentered the workforce, I thought I was ready for anything, that the peace of mind I had achieved would see me through whatever came my way. And for a while it did. But nine months later I found myself again absorbed in my job, making it and the money I made and the relationships I had or didn't have much too important. I woke up one morning and noticed that my mind was again noisy and that I was depressed much too often. I had once again, somewhere, lost the joy of living. So I took a vacation to the desert to look at my life and to decide what was next. While there, I realized that my serenity was compromised because I had expected the five months at the monastery to somehow carry me through the rest of my life. And although I was still meditating now and then, I realized that I needed to include some form of the practice in every day. I needed to structure my time in a better way. I needed to take better care of myself and do things that were spiritually satisfying. I needed to find a quiet corner in my life. And I needed to write about it, for myself and, hopefully, for others. Out of this was born my first book, *Find a Quiet Corner—A Simple Guide to Self-Peace*. I learned how to find the time in my hectic life to meditate, how important it is to be fully awake and mindful in every moment, and how to find serenity in each day. I do not need to retreat to the top of a mountain—this peace is available to me every moment, wherever I am.

The patterns that we establish early operate throughout our lives unless we become aware of them and take some actions to change them. Yet even after our awareness comes, these patterns often continue to subtly operate without our blessing. They are so integrated into our behavior and belief system that we resort to them reflexively, without thinking. For myself, I recognized a pattern that often appeared after I had accomplished something. After publication of *Find a Quiet Corner*, I noticed that I again felt like I could coast, just like when I returned from the monastery. Once again, I figured I was set. My life from then on would be calm, serene, spiritually "right." I could stroll down the road of my life toward enlightenment. I was entitled to the easier, softer way. I had worked hard and deserved these rewards.

But my life didn't get less rocky. In fact, it got more difficult to manage. My job got bigger and more demanding. I was away from home much too often. I had little time for my spiritual work, for family, for friends. And writing—which had become an activity that I finally admitted was essential to satisfy my creative heart center—was all too often put on the back burner or at the bottom of my priority list.

That's when I came to realize something that led me to write *Just Listen:* serenity alone is not enough—inner peace is but the beginning of a truly contented and emotionally balanced life. We need to become quiet and still so that we can listen, so that we can hear our true inner voice. We need to become quiet and still so that the divine can have an opportunity to enter our lives. The stillness and the silence are necessary to bring us back to ourselves.

My inner voice was telling me to take a big risk, to quit my job. In hanging on to this job I was still listening to what others were saying and still looking outside myself for satisfaction and approval. Even though I had written a book, my job continued to define who I was to some extent, and it also drained me, taking away my time to do anything else. I wanted to spend more time with my family and friends, I wanted to remember and mark their birthdays, to enjoy my time with them, and to have time for myself. My inner voice was telling me to take the risk, to leave the job, to trust that I'd be okay. My true voice was speaking to me loud and clear, and because of all the work I had done since my father's death, I heard it. I did not know exactly how I would support myself; I only knew that my job zapped my creative and spiritual energy and that writing released it. I had to believe that by following the path that fulfilled me, the bills would get paid. Besides, I reminded myself, I could always get another job if things didn't work out. The realization here was that all will be revealed. The answers are in the silence.

Most of us live our lives the same way I had been living before I woke up from my half-dream state. We feel like there's something missing from our lives; we feel at times empty and unfulfilled. If we pause to consider why this might be, we feel as though time is not on our side, that there just isn't enough of it, and that we'll never figure it out. We end up regretting the past and having no hope for the future. We then resign ourselves to our lives and fall back into our half-dream state toward our inevitable end, or we sink into a state of despair where we can see no light. In either case, we live in negativity, where the joy of life cannot reach us.

The process that awakens us from our half-dream state is elucidated here in *Just Listen*. If followed, it will help you to eliminate the negativity in your life. It will teach you how to discover and enjoy each moment. It will make you feel more alive than ever as you learn to fully experience everything that comes your way—the pain as well as the joy. The exercises suggested here can be implemented and practiced daily. They will put you in touch with yourself in a way you've never experienced. You will gain greater appreciation for the small gifts in your life and learn to trust your gut instincts.

Many spiritual disciplines use the word *path* or *way* to define the course of their teachings. In *Just Listen* I describe a path that can bring you to a place of emotional balance and spiritual serenity. A path that will imbue your daily life with joy, that will teach you about love and intimacy. A path that will give you the resources to deal with the changing circumstances of your life without resistance. I refer to this as the *Quiet Corner* path, which you can take to find your inner voice and gain serenity.

Read through the book first without expecting anything of yourself. This will give you an overview of the whole process and the rewards that await you. But don't feel daunted by the enormity of it all. Simply go back to the beginning and take it one page, one step at a time. Taken that way, none of this will overwhelm you, you will reap the benefits, and that empty, unfulfilled feeling will slip away. Keep in mind that all these things are merely suggestions. Take from here what suits you and your particular personality; discard the rest. I would suggest, though, that you give it all a try before you make the decision to ignore any of it. Only then will you know what fits and what doesn't. This is your life, your path, and it is up to you to design it and construct the scenery. In *Just Listen* I share with you how I discovered my voice and how you can discover yours. I introduce techniques you can use to hear and trust your voice. You will be rewarded by tapping into it.

I no longer need disasters to wake up my spirit. I no longer need earth-shattering events like death and devastating pain to initiate change. I no longer want that kind of drama. I now see the warning signs of confusion and distress long before they are on my doorstep. My creative spirit is fully awake as a result of my experiences over the past twelve years. I am living the life I thought was reserved for only the truly blessed. I have given up the security of a regular paycheck for the security of spiritual abundance.

Please come along and discover that you, too, are truly blessed and deserve nothing less than what the *Quiet Corner* path will bring you. Come along and learn how to listen to your true self.

BOOK I

Becoming Aware

~~~~~~~~~~~

Situating
Yourself

WHAT IS OUR PURPOSE HERE?

Like everyone else, you probably are searching for something in this life to satisfy a dream, a longing, or something that you can't even name. As you begin to read this book you may even have an agenda for yourself. Perhaps you're looking for answers to the gnawing questions in your brain about what your role in this life is. And perhaps you're looking for some serenity, a little peace of mind that will at least temporarily take you away from your troubles. Maybe you've tried other things to help you gain this peace and nothing has worked, so you're skeptical that anything can work.

Perhaps you've reached some measure of peace in your life and want to go deeper. You want to experience more joy. You want to experience your life more fully, and you want to achieve an emotional balance so that the highs and lows of life are moderated.

Or maybe you're committed to the pursuit of happiness at any cost, or to acquiring things like money and power because you believe that these will give you joy and freedom.

Perhaps you don't even know what you want—you just know

that something is amiss, something needs to happen inside you because no matter what happens to and around you there is no satisfaction. Maybe you have everything you've ever dreamed of—the compatible relationship, the satisfying job, the nice home, plenty of love from children and family—yet something inside feels empty. You might even hesitate to acknowledge this empty feeling, thinking that your friends and family wouldn't believe you or would consider you ungrateful.

Perhaps you believe you have a fatal flaw that nothing and nobody can correct, and up to this point in your life you've kept it your secret. Or maybe you're sitting with a minor under-the-skin-dis-ease, something you can live with but that colors the way you see everything. It's not extreme, mostly it goes unnoticed by others, but it's beginning to affect your behavior more and more. You're simply fed up with it and want it gone.

Right now, try not to figure any of this out, and don't worry about where or whether you fit in to any of these scenarios. Simply know that wherever you are coming from and wherever you think you might want to go, you are, right this moment, in the right place. Know that whatever you think your purpose in life or your purpose in reading this book is, you are, right this moment, in the right place.

Let's make a pact. Let's agree that for now our purpose is to be present and willing, right here, right now. To this end, let's do a simple exercise. Look around you. What does the room you're in look like? Are there windows? Notice the source of light. What shoes are you wearing? Are you standing or sitting? How's your breathing? Take three long, deep breaths to put your attention there. Look around you again. Ground yourself in the here and now. Focus on just being where you are, right now, in this moment. Breathe deeply.

This exercise is a simple one, and I will ask you to remember it and turn to it from time to time. Let's call it your *purpose tool.* Whenever you find yourself fearful or anxious, use this tool. Whenever the question "What is my purpose?" arises, use this tool. Whenever you are in a state of existential angst, use this tool. Whenever you don't know what to do next, use this tool.

You may be asking yourself such questions as "Why? What good will this do me? How can such a simple exercise help with the important matters of my life?" Take a moment. Stop. Use your purpose tool. If you practice this regularly and follow the other suggestions in this book, I promise that you will find the answers to even your most perplexing questions. But for now let's agree that our purpose is to be here, on this page, in this moment, and nowhere else. That is enough purpose just now. Read along, trust, and bring this tool with you as you go.

Throughout the *Quiet Corner* process we will be studying our mind. We will see how it controls us and learn to what extent we have control over it. Being human, most of us have very active minds. Generally, we just accept this as normal and may not even realize that much of our stress and anxiety comes from our busy minds. Have you ever paid attention to what your mind actually contains? When we sit quietly alone with ourselves we can begin to hear what's there inside us, and the point of doing this is to clear our minds of empty chatter and hear the deep, inner truth of ourselves. But before we explore that, let's look at what a busy mind might contain and feel like.

A busy mind might contain thoughts of what you have to do later this afternoon, tomorrow, or next week. It might be thinking about yesterday's meeting with the boss and trying to figure out what he's thinking or what his next move will be. Maybe it dreams about last week's date or next month's vacation as you pretend to pay attention to what you're doing at the moment. Thoughts of bills waiting to be paid sit in one corner of your brain, while thoughts of where you'll be picking up the kids, how you're going to afford your mother's nursing home, and when your best friend will be out of the hospital invade the other corners. A busy mind can jump from one thought to the next, spanning years, without your even noticing the shift.

A busy mind can keep you awake at night with feelings, unresolved dilemmas, worries, hopes, and fears. A busy mind can so preoccupy you that accidents happen. It might cause such anxiety that your physical health becomes weakened. A busy mind can torment you to distraction and leave you feeling helpless, hopeless, and empty. A busy mind might all at once start telling you how to do things, what not to do, when to do it, whom to or not to do it with, how you should look, what you should think about this or that, what you could have said to avoid this morning's argument, what to cook for dinner. Your busy mind might ask those tormenting who-what-when questions ad nauseam. What will happen at tomorrow's job interview? Will I have enough money to pay the rent? Will my job be the next to go? Does he (or she) like me? When will I see him again? This goes on until you think you might explode from the sheer weight of words floating around in your head. There are enough voices to supply a choir and then some.

You might be asking yourself "What can I possibly gain from finding my true inner voice? I have enough voices in my head, I don't need to find another one." While reading this book, put aside such questions. Let's practice taking them (and all judgments and criticisms) as they arise and putting them aside. When such a question comes up, write it on a slip of paper and put it away. You may want to start an envelope or a box or drawer in which to collect these slips of paper. Believe it or not, by the time you finish this book, if you are diligent about taking the suggestions here, you will see that all your questions will either be answered or will have become irrelevant. So write them down and put them away for now.

When we get right down to it and actually notice the various components and voices that contribute to our busy mind, we realize that much of it is repetitive and mundane. Our minds usually are not cluttered with creative ideas that stem from our genius. Generally, our thoughts deal with the boring specifics of our day-to-day lives or with abstract philosophical questions that we'll never resolve. Sometimes we compartmentalize the different parts of our busy mind to avoid too much conflict and competition among them. Yet, though we try our best, they often struggle to have their say, keeping us awake at night or interfering each time we are about to make a big decision. And these parts of our mind do not cancel each other out. They rarely agree, a situation that usually just leads us to more confusion. Rarely does such a busy mind live in harmony. It can often rule our lives without us even knowing it.

If none of this applies to you, that's great, you're a rare individual. But most of us have extremely active minds. Some of us have a high tolerance for the noise, while others let it get the best of us, adding to our stress and making us unable to focus and think clearly. We all differ in how we deal with our mind noise. And there's no point in trying to figure out how someone else's mind behaves. Trying to compare ourselves with others is a frustrating and fruitless mind game. So begin by becoming aware of and accepting your own unique and wonderful mind just as it is. Resist the impulse to compare.

If your mind is a busy one and you'd like to learn how to calm it down, you can take steps to do so. The first thing you can do is simply observe your mind as it works. Start paying closer attention. What are you thinking of right now? Jot it down. Keep it simple. Next? Where did it go from there? Jot that down. Imagine that you have volume and channel selector knobs in your brain. Place them wherever you'd like. Behind your eyes. In the back of your throat. At the crown of your head. Now close your eyes and breathe. As one thought pops up, notice it and play with your dials. Turn up the volume. Change the channel and go to another thought. Now turn it down. Notice that I didn't suggest an on/off switch. That is because your mind is permanently on. But there are control switches you can learn how to use.

So accept your mind as it is, know that you are, right now, powerless over the noise, and trust that there is a solution, that serenity and a peaceful mind are possible.

MIND NOISE

Once you start to become aware and take note of what your mind is doing, create a *Quiet Corner* bank in which to store all your questions, self-judgments, and self-criticisms. Perhaps you could make something out of construction paper. Make it colorful and big enough to hold many slips of paper. Don't try to imagine how many questions you might ask yourself before the questions slow down. You can always make a second or third or fourth container if the first becomes too small. Have some fun. Make a game of it. Use magazines or old newspapers or even an empty coffee can. Paint it, decorate it, label it. And then put it away. Let it be the vessel for your nagging questions. This is the beginning of clearing your head of some of the noise so that you can begin to hear your inner voice. Be aware that once you write a question down and put it in the bank, it may revisit you. That's okay and perfectly natural. Simply write it down again and redeposit it. There may be something to learn from the repetition.

THE AHA! EXPERIENCE

As we go along, I will make suggestions of things to do that will help you along your path. So far I've suggested that you

1. Carry with you and use your "purpose tool,"
2. Observe your mind as it works,
3. Write down your mind questions (and judgments and criticisms), and
4. Make a mind question bank.

A lot of suggestions just to begin! If you're anything like me, you might judge them as silly and inconsequential or resist doing them at all. At first glance, many of the suggestions in this book will seem slight and meaningless, but try to think of them as a grocery list. Before you go shopping you know what you have and what you need, but a list is always helpful in assisting you in your chore; it helps you to remember all that you need and to avoid buying things you don't need. A list may seem unnecessary (you have it all in your head), but it can be useful. And while each ingredient you buy is not always or necessarily a meal in itself, it will combine with other ingredients to form a perfect meal. That's how you can look at each suggestion here—as just one ingredient to be included in a life of serenity.

You can also look at these suggestions as nuggets of surprise. Until you actually do them, break open their shell, you can't know what's waiting for you inside. If you've ever discovered or learned something in an indirect way (in trying to solve one problem, the answer to another is revealed), you've had the *aha! experience*. So keep an open mind as you approach the suggestions because they have the potential to work this way. And each one will reveal a secret just for you.

As you become aware of your busy mind, one exercise might help before you look closer and deal with what's actually there. You can do this exercise to give yourself a break from the din and to create some space so that you can approach and absorb the suggestions here. You can do it not only now, at the beginning of your journey, but at various points along the way when things get to be a little too much to handle comfortably. It does not offer a long-term solution to busy mind, but it introduces some temporary peace. As you move along the *Quiet Corner* path, taking the suggestions here, your mind will gradually become quieter and more serene. A time will come when you no longer need this exercise. But in the meantime, use it when your stress level is high or when you can't sleep at night for all the voices and the who-what-when questions yapping at you. Or use it as a daily exercise until you achieve permanent quietness of mind.

Find a relatively quiet place where you can be alone and sit undisturbed for a half-hour or so. Bring your purpose tool with you and ground yourself in the here and now. Pay attention to the space around you and the way your body is feeling. Then sit comfortably, close your eyes, and take three deep, full breaths. Notice how you're breathing. Then visualize your mind (or your brain center) and imagine that you can see all the various aspects that contribute to the noise there. Begin to isolate each one. Give each a shape, a name. Don't judge. Don't criticize or blame. Don't analyze. Just observe.

Each time you identify a voice and name it, make it as small as possible. See it shrink in your mind and become just dust or ashes. Put it in a corner and move to the next voice and the next and the next, until you've identified and shrunk everything that crops up during this session. Then imagine this pile of ashes being swept up and thrown out. Imagine a gentle wind collecting it into a vortex and sweeping it out of your mind, through the crown of your head. Then imagine these ashes being blown into some sort of vessel for safekeeping. You might want to have with you a favorite bowl, vase, or box in which to deposit them. When you're finished with the exercise, set this container alongside your *Quiet Corner* question bank and use it each time you practice this exercise.

Now, sit quietly and breathe. Take three long, deep breaths and just concentrate on your breath. How do you feel? Is your breathing any different now after this exercise? Don't think too much. Give your brain a rest. Relax. Just breathe.

Now, do something nice for yourself. Go buy yourself some flowers or a book of poems. Sit in a garden or by a stream. Play with your dog or cat. Pick your child up early from school and play in the park, or go by yourself and sit in a swing. Just breathe, take a break, a long walk around the neighborhood. Pretend that you don't have a brain for the rest of the day. Go out for dinner or let someone else cook. Don't make any decisions. Care for yourself as you would a newborn. Be gentle and loving. Don't worry, you will think again, and only too soon. For now, though, enjoy the luxury of no-brain existence and just breathe in the glory of life. Trust that this exercise will make you more aware of what is in your mind—what can easily go, what you hold on to, and how much of what is there is uniquely your own. Your voice will slowly begin to whisper its presence to you, and you will begin to hear it.

MIND ASHES

Making the container for your brain's ashes can be another fun project. If you're handy with wood you might construct a box that suits your particular taste. Let your imagination run amok. If you knit, a wild-colored stocking with a flapped closure could be fun. If you want to make something but haven't a clue where to begin, ask your children or a friend to help. Make a family project out of it. Or designate an old jewelry box or new coffee mug for your ashes. Be inventive. Be creative. Because you are.

Once you start clearing your mind of your nagging mind questions and storing them away, you will begin to be ready to identify your quiet voice. It may have been so quiet over the years that it has become lost. But it wants you to discover it, nurture it, bring it back to life. It needs you, and you need it. For without this voice we become stuck in our bodies, automatons, out of touch with both our inner and outer worlds. This voice is the thread that connects us to ourselves and to the world. Without it, we are cut off.

Many of us have been taught to mind a different voice—the voice that is in our heads, the voice that is judgmental and scared. Perhaps it is the voice of your father, a teacher, or a priest. Most likely your voice has become an amalgam of many others. Chances are it is restrictive, unfeeling, uncaring, concerned about dire consequences, an echo of past experiences, a representation of old attitudes that are not organic to you but adopted from others.

Throughout this book we will work toward squashing the voices that don't belong to you. We will identify them and exorcise the ones that hold you back, that muffle your true voice, that interfere with your unique expression. Some of these voices are cunning and will at first seem to belong to you, or you'll find that you've become so attached to some that you're unwilling to let them go. But slowly, over time, if you follow the suggestions here, you will clear your mind, open your heart, and return to yourself.

My friend Ruth had a voice inside pushing her to pursue her Ph.D. She struggled for years on this course, convincing herself that she must be "less than" other people on the same track because it was taking longer than "normal" and she wasn't having any fun. She blamed herself, unable to see that getting her Ph.D. was not her vision at all but one that had been thrust upon her by her parents. Her father has a doctorate in physics, her mother, a master's in modern dance, and they encouraged Ruth in many different ways to follow their lead. Ruth remembers her mother telling her at sixteen, when she felt awkward in social situations, not to worry, that "it will be so much better when you get to graduate school." It was always assumed she would go.

Ruth's discontentment and unease with higher learning had nothing to do with her capabilities or intelligence. She was always a good student. She is bright, energetic, and curious. And her academic achievements—she has a master's in German literature and was well along on the doctorate road—confirmed her parents' wishes for her and convinced her that her fate was academia. This idea was further entrenched when she met her husband. His vision of them as a couple only served to solidify the course she was on. He saw them as parallel intellectual companions—professors teaching their respective courses, discussing their academic pursuits, and moving along together toward similar goals.

It wasn't that any of these people meant badly. They all thought they were supporting Ruth in what she wanted. But, as she now says, "Just because you're good at something doesn't mean it is what you should be doing. In fact, it might be better to pursue something that you might not be so good at but that fulfills you more emotionally."

One day after talking it over with many people whom she trusted and loved, and after working through many of the issues associated with this pursuit, Ruth decided to quit her Ph.D. program. Today she is happier than ever working at a job she loves that affords her time to express herself artistically in dance and knitting. She discovered that, though she was smart academically, expressing herself creatively satisfied her on a much deeper, spiritual level. Had she continued to listen to the voices that weren't her own she might still be struggling toward someone else's goal, never able to express her unique and impressive talents.

Ruth's decision to leave academia did not mean she had to leave her family—she is still happily married to her husband and expecting a child this year. When we reject someone else's vision for us, it does not mean that we have to reject that someone. In fact, listening to ourselves and following our heart usually serves to bring us closer to others.

Take a few minutes now and think about where you are in your life, where you want to be, and whose dream you are living. No need to do anything yet. Maybe you have your dream job, maybe you practice a craft that fulfills you, or maybe you haven't even a clue about what you might enjoy doing. In any case, the first step in getting to know yourself better and to know what moves and enriches you is noticing that you want to go deeper into yourself and get to the true you. No need to expect anything more of yourself right now. This awareness is enough.

One valuable activity that you will be encouraged to do throughout this book is writing things down. This helps to get rid of the surface noise, get to the crux of things, and achieve heightened awareness. Just as a blind person must touch objects to "see" them, even after he is given back his sight, so we must "touch" our thoughts and feelings to understand them. Writing is a powerful way to get in touch with and see our inner self.

So begin to write your history and what you hope to gain from this book. Why are you now willing to look at your life? Are you willing to look? Write about whatever is currently in the forefront of your mind, how you feel about where you are right now in your life, what you might like to change in your life, and your fears about all of it. Try not to edit yourself as you go along. No one else need read what you write. This is for your eyes only. Trust in yourself, in the process, and attempt to be honest. As long as you are willing—not perfect, just willing—you have all that is necessary to get started. Think about being available for

yourself and your life. Your world will never be the same again—
it will be better.

YOUR QUIET CORNER PLACE

Since you will be writing a lot as you progress on this quest of
finding your own voice, you may want to dedicate a special notebook and pen for your *Quiet Corner* exercises. You might also
want to dedicate a drawer or shelf for keeping all the various
Quiet Corner paraphernalia that you accumulate on this journey.
There won't be an enormous quantity of things, as we try on this
path to be free of clutter, but you'll gather a few things that will
relate to your *Quiet Corner* experience and that you will need for
the suggested exercises. Assigning a special *Quiet Corner* place will
simply confirm your commitment and honor your dedication to
your spiritual path.

Often the hardest thing about starting anything new, challenging, or creative, like embarking on this *Quiet Corner* journey, is simply that—starting. Our mind, our doubts, our fears, the loud voices within us, our judge and critic, keep us from even trying. In my case, I liken it to my resistance to physical exercise. The most difficult part is putting on my workout clothes and walking out the door. Once I make it that far, the rest is easy. I always enjoy it, I always feel better. Yet I resist it the very next time. Why? Because I tend to resist most activities that are beneficial to my health. So knowing this about myself helps to push me out the door each time.

I have been involved in routine physical activity for many years and have come to understand and accept my various moods and limitations in that arena. I can sometimes work out with unlimited energy and grace, while at other times I feel sluggish and bored. For stretches of time I exercise every chance I get; at other times I don't exercise at all. I no longer allow any of this to persuade me that I should either be a professional athlete or that I should never exercise again. My particular body simply works this way, and I have come to know just when to push myself and when to hold back. I no longer judge or compare myself with others; I just accept my physical being as it is.

Such seemingly minor realizations can increase our self-awareness and help us to identify similar patterns in other areas of our life that affect our mental and spiritual well-being. Have you ever constructed in your mind an ideal you? Do you put pressure on yourself to conform to this image? Write down some examples of how you do this. Then consider that this pressure could be keeping you from approaching new and creative endeavors, since you have an established idea of the outcome before you even begin. And nothing, good or bad, ever turns out the way we imagine it. Getting started and leaving behind all expectations is always a challenge. When you have trouble getting started doing anything, remind yourself that once you take the first step you are on your way. Choose one small action that will get you moving. If I resist beginning a new writing project, for instance, I know that picking up my pen and notebook or sitting down in front of my computer and turning it on is similar to walking out the door. Yet it sometimes takes a while to get there. I circle the computer, thinking about being there, worrying about being there, wanting to be there. This is all part of the process that eventually gets me there. I now accept this. And I always get there.

Pay attention to your own particular patterns as you work on becoming more aware. Do you routinely resist some activity even though you enjoy it once you get started? What pushes you to do it each time? What is your version of walking out the door? Make a list of activities that you once enjoyed but no longer practice. Would you like to introduce some of them back into your life? What would it take to do that? Write down three activities that you've only ever dreamed of doing or admired from afar. Write down three or more professions that you would like to try your hand at. No need to take action on any of this yet; simply write about it all for now in your *Quiet Corner* notebook. Consider these your "life's dreams" pages. And remember that whenever you are having trouble getting started doing something new, especially something creative, start by doing something small, something that feels easy and manageable, to get you through that door of resistance. For example, if you think you'd like to return to school but are worried about not having the resources (time, money, skill), start simply by collecting catalogs from the schools that interest you. Start there. Then maybe make a phone call to the one that most interests you and inquire further about the schedule or fees. Or, if you decide that you want to make a quilt, first get a book on the subject, then research local quilting groups, then perhaps begin a small project before you determine your long-term interest or talent. Focusing on these small steps will move you in some direction. And each step will take you further along the road. So, don't jump to the end of whatever it is you want to do before you get there. Just push yourself into that mental space of willingness, through that imaginary door, and take one small action. The end will take care of itself. Before you know it, you will have started. That is the hard part. Once you're there, you're there.

While much of what we do to be in tune with our own true voice involves action, the most important activity appears on the surface to be one of nonaction. Yet it is the key that unlocks our hearts and minds and awakens our voice. This activity is, simply, just sitting. Sitting quietly and concentrating on your breath—this is the cornerstone of *Quiet Corner* practice, from which all else flows. So incorporate some *Quiet Corner* sitting into your daily schedule and prepare yourself for some quiet miracles.

The first thing to do (this will appeal to all of you who feel you must always be doing something) is to find a space in your home for sitting. A section of the floor with cushions is ideal, but if that does not work for you a chair can be just as effective. You need to find a position that keeps your spine erect and allows your breath to flow easily. If you choose the floor, sit cross-legged, with your buttocks propped up on one or two cushions so that your butt and your knees form a tripod to support your body. Your tummy should be pushed slightly forward, with your spine perfectly erect and your hands clasped gently in your lap. If you choose a chair, make it a straight-back chair and not one that you will sink into. Sit on a small, flat cushion with your tummy relaxed and your spine upright. Then place both feet flat on the floor and gently clasp your hands in your lap. Do this in bare or stockinged feet and place a small cushion under them if that is more comfortable. Keep in mind that each of us has a natural curve to our spine, we're not attempting to achieve a straight spine here, just an erect one. Now you are ready to sit.

Bring your attention to your breath. Notice your inhalation and your exhalation. Count each exhalation up to ten, and then begin again. Keep your eyes gently open so as not to fall asleep or daydream. Gaze softly at a spot just above the floor, about three feet in front of you, with nothing in sharp focus. And just concentrate on your breath. Your thoughts will not cease. This is perfectly normal. Just let your thoughts be thoughts and your breath be breath. Let your thoughts float by without following them. Just breathe. If you lose your count, begin again. If counting to three works better for you, then count to three. If counting each inhalation and each exhalation works for you, then do that. There are no rules here except to sit and breathe. You will develop your own style—whatever works to keep you sitting and concentrating on your breath.

Don't be too strict with yourself as you begin sitting, but as you grow more accustomed to the activity try to move less and less during each session. Begin slowly with ten minutes each day and gradually increase that to twenty, then to thirty or forty-five minutes. Don't rush it. Don't push yourself so fast that you stop altogether. Know your limitations and accept them. Be gentle with yourself. The rewards of sitting will be yours if you follow the suggestions here. The physical act of sitting completely still may seem awkward, painful, and even ludicrous at first. But if you make the attempt, you will learn a great deal about yourself and your world. The physical discomfort that you may experience will focus your attention on your physical pain and away from the chatter in your head. Your mind obsessions will stop as you become aware of your body. And then, if you just breathe into your pain, it will lessen. Your mind, body, and spirit will become calm. You will just breathe and sit still in the quiet of your being, open and ready to hear your own true voice.

YOUR QUIET CORNER

Just as you have set aside a small space in your home for your *Quiet Corner* paraphernalia—notebooks, question bank, mind ashes container—you might think about setting aside a larger space in which to spend your *Quiet Corner* time. Perhaps you could make some pillows of your own to put in this space or designate a special chair just for *Quiet Corner* sitting. If you cannot set up a permanent space as yours, create a *Quiet Corner* space each time you retreat to it. By using a special piece of fabric, a favorite scarf or shawl, some cushions, along with candles and incense, you will immediately transform the everyday into the sacred. A *Quiet Corner* space is possible anywhere. You needn't limit yourself just to the place you set up at home. While it may be impractical to carry cushions and incense with you every day, you can certainly bring such things with you on vacations or overnight business trips. And during your everyday life there are plenty of opportunities to grab some *Quiet Corner* time even if your tools are not accessible. Commuting to and from work, sitting in the doctor's waiting room, rocking your child to sleep at night, spending lunchtime in your office with the door closed or in a nearby church or park—your *Quiet Corner* is transportable. Be imaginative. Be resourceful. Because you are.

⑥ CENTERING

Our intention on the *Quiet Corner* path is to free our inner voice and move toward spontaneity and creative expression. But first it is important to create some structure, which will help our voice and encourage and support our endeavor. Having a structure will first ground you and then allow you to soar to new heights.

We will be returning to four key elements in this *Quiet Corner* process:

- ⑥ Sitting and breathing
- ⑥ Writing things down
- ⑥ Talking to someone else
- ⑥ Moving our bodies

For the moment, let's look at just one of them—sitting and breathing. While all four activities are centering ones, this one helps us to center all the rest. This one will teach us the most about *just listening*. It is the simplest but certainly not the easiest step. But it is the easiest to ignore. And this is the one that we absolutely must not ignore.

The best way to not ignore this exercise is to set up a structure for it. Schedule it into your day. Create a *Quiet Corner* in your home. Plan it as you would any other activity, or you may never do it. If you don't set aside some time to sit quietly and breathe, you will find that this time will become filled with something else. Even once you know how beneficial it is to sit and breathe, don't assume that you will do it without scheduling it in. Whenever you are off-center, unbalanced, or too involved with the noise in your head, consider whether you have been delinquent in setting time aside to just sit. This is likely the case, so make a point to schedule it. Or, before long, you will be far away from your true self and into the obsessions and delusions of your ordinary mind.

So do yourself a favor and set some time aside for this most centering of activities. Once a day, twice a week. Structure it so that it is doable, and then do it. As you read this, bring your attention to your breath. As you breathe in, be aware that you are breathing in. As you breathe out, be aware that you are breathing out. In. Out. Simple. Centering.

2

Seeing the Big Picture

KNOWING WHAT YOU WANT

Before you can get what you want you have to know what you want. That may sound obvious, but how many times have you been hungry and not known what you wanted to eat? Sometimes, we just don't know. It may be easy to admit it when it comes to food, but there are other hungers that we may have that we don't have a clue how to satisfy. The first step then is to identify the hunger, for only then can we determine how to feed it.

We are inundated these days with information telling us what we are supposed to want. You can't walk down the street without being bombarded with some message or another—on the sides of buses, on T-shirts, in store windows. Would we even know how to dress without fashion magazines, advertisements, peer pressure? I often used to find myself looking to others before I could decide what to purchase, even when it came to something as simple as the color of my lipstick. Yet over and over and over again I notice that the things I am happiest with are those I select on my own, those that are not influenced by fashion or someone else's taste. Many of the messages are so subtle that I can't even be sure they are my decisions, made to please only me. And if it is this confusing to know what material things we want, no wonder we have difficulty becoming aware of the intangible things we want in life.

From the time we are young, incredible pressure is put on us to conform to the norms that have been established by those before us. All my life I felt like I wasn't doing it right, like I didn't fit in. It was as though there was this huge game going on and I was never given a set of instructions on how to play. For many years I hunted and searched for those rules, in all the wrong places and to no avail. Today I no longer need to live by someone else's rules. I've stopped looking for a rescuer. I no longer try to make myself fit into someone else's idea of myself. I am now free to explore all the subtleties of my being. And I have come to see that when this is painful it is merely the pain that comes with being human. I've discovered that this pain is often the inspiration for growth.

Write down where you would like to be in a year and what you think you want in your life. Be specific and realistic. Now write down the dreams and fantasies that you have for your life. Be honest and true to yourself. Be imaginative, but don't make things up that don't fit just to write something down. If you have no dreams, write about that. Having no dreams and fantasies is as legitimate at this point as living in a dream world.

Now place these written testimonies in an envelope and seal it. Label it "Dreams/Desires/Fantasies" and date it. Put it on your *Quiet Corner* altar and forget about it for now. Then turn your attention back to the process you've begun here. Take the next step along the *Quiet Corner* path, which will guide you toward your true self. And then take the next step and the next. If you continue along the path outlined here, you might be surprised at the outcome, though it will work much better if you can forget about that for now. Simply show up for yourself each day and participate in your life. Do what is required of you to achieve daily peace of mind. And then, little by little, gifts will begin to manifest. If you are prepared and fully awake to them, you will see how they surpass anything you might have thought you wanted for yourself.

Stay on the path, and then open your envelope a year later. One of two things will become evident. Either you will see all your dreams, and more, realized, or you will decide that what you thought you wanted for yourself was indeed limiting, you will be grateful for how your life has taken shape, and glad that you didn't get only what you asked for. In either case, if you are truly on your *Quiet Corner* path, you will see that a force is working in your life that is beyond your rational mind's grasp. You will see that if you define what you want simply as personal spiritual progress, then you will get everything you need.

⑥ FEAR

Fear can be one of our biggest obstacles as we move through life. It can loom so large that we actually avoid much of our life, or at least the aspects of it that give it color and meaning. Often we are unaware of just how much fear rules our life. Generally, all our fears stem from a self-centered place, from the big fear that something bad will happen to us, that we will somehow be hurt or, worse, embarrassed. Many of us also fear that we will not get what we want and will lose what we have. So we protect ourselves and build up our defenses so much that we limit our lives. Some of our fears are based in reality but then move into other spheres, infecting our vision, our behavior, our attitudes. Say, for example, you were bitten by a dog as a child. This might have caused you to shy away from all dogs at that time and to see all dogs as threatening and potentially evil, which caused you to avoid areas where dogs might be. Because you were able to arrange your life to be free of dogs, this fear could be forgotten. But in living with this fear you missed out on the joy and love that being around dogs can engender. And maybe as an adult this fear influences you in such a way that you don't jog in unfamiliar neighborhoods even though jogging is your latest passion. You make excuses and let this fear, which may no longer even be connected to the dog bite, determine your movements. Your world gets smaller and smaller, your range of motion limited by this fear.

While this example may not apply to you, it serves to illustrate how powerful and far-reaching our fears can be. We will look at our fears in more detail later on, but for now just begin to become aware of what scares you. We will learn that the only way to conquer fear is to face it. And we will see that, once faced, no fear is as scary as our imagination makes it seem. We will also learn that some of our richest and most spiritually rewarding moments come when we've looked into the abyss of fear that we've been ignoring.

Although the dictionary tells us that courage is what allows us to face difficulty, pain, and danger without fear, it also takes courage to face our fears. They are not easy to look at, let alone approach, but if we don't face them they will continue to control our lives. And by facing fear I don't mean jumping into the deep end of the pool if you're afraid of water. Simply admit this fear into your consciousness and then maybe take swimming lessons. Gradually, if you move closer to what frightens you, it will appear smaller and less threatening, and you will pick up tools along the way that will help you manage your fear. All of this takes courage. And at some point you will move through the world with little or no fear left, and the word *courage* will be used by others to describe you. When you hear yourself being referred to as courageous, you won't quite understand at first because the actions you are taking in your life, for the very first time, will feel normal, natural, and right. Then one day you will realize that those calling you courageous are still swimming in fear and that somewhere along the path you have lost yours. So muster up the courage to face your fears and this will lead you to a life without fear, where you will face all the pain and difficulty that life sends your way, fearlessly and with great courage.

I have never scuba dived, but I dreamt about it one night. The whole idea of strapping an oxygen tank onto my back and diving deep into the fathomless ocean terrifies, yet also excites, me on a gut level. In the dream, each time I was about to submerge myself and plunge into the depths, I would hold my breath as though I were simply ducking my head under water with no air supply other than my previous breath. I kept forgetting, and was gently reminded by a gentle soul who was with me in the dream, that I did not have to hold my breath, I just had to continue breathing normally. I was carrying my air supply on my back and could simply breathe as usual. This image is a good one to remember whenever we are about to plunge into a depth that arouses fear. Whenever we find ourselves holding our breath, it may be that we are unconsciously fearful. No need to hold our breath. No need to worry. We will be fine. We have all the tools we need. We must simply continue to breathe normally and pay attention to the scenery. Fear is okay. Not breathing is not okay. So strap on your air supply each time you are frightened, and jump in. Your breath will guide you and see you through.

NIGHT DREAMS

Do you recall your dreams after waking each morning? Or do they slip away unremembered? Do you often have the hazy sense that you've dreamt something but can't quite grasp any of the details? We all have dreams, whether we remember them or not, and they can be important tools for honing awareness and getting to our true, uninhibited, authentic self.

If you have trouble recalling your dreams, each night before going to sleep say to yourself: "I want to remember my dreams." Say this three times. You will be surprised how effective this simple exercise is. You will begin to remember your dreams. It may not work perfectly and may not work always, but it will work often enough.

Then begin to jot down your dreams, or the fragments that you remember. And to your nightly chant add: "I want to write them down." Three times. This will help you to remember to pick up your pen before you do anything else.

Keep a pad and pen next to your bed, and write about your dreams as soon as you wake up. Don't even get out of bed. Otherwise, you may risk losing them. It doesn't take much time, and you may be surprised about your inner, subconscious world.

Once you start this you might notice images and words popping up in the middle of the day from one of your dreams. Quick, write them down. Later we will talk more specifically about how these dreams can inform your spiritual practice. For now, just dream away and treasure them by recording them.

Were you a happy teenager? Did you like and trust people? If you were anything like me and many other people I know, the answer to these questions would be a resounding NO. When I was a teenager, I had decided that other people, especially adults, could not be trusted or relied upon and that relying on no one was the only solution to a bad situation. So I turned my back on other people and became a self-sufficient, totally independent young woman. Many teenagers adopt this attitude but drop it as they get older. I, however, continued this defiant stance into adulthood, and it served me well for many years. Or so I thought. Not until my life came crashing down around me when my father died, and I needed to reach out for help, did I realize how utterly alone and lonely I had become. How hard it was for me to ask for help. I didn't even know whom to ask it of, but I knew that if I didn't, I might as well give up living entirely.

So I began to take baby steps with this reaching out business. It's a good idea to start with something small whenever you must take a 360-degree turn in life. Or when you are about to explore new and personally untested territory. When I first set out on my new course, one small step that I took was to talk to other people who were dealing with similar issues. I wasn't yet ready to reach out to my family, so I sought out support groups and committed myself to at least attempting to practice some of their suggestions to conquer and make peace with my fears. I was told that I had to keep the focus on myself for a while, that I couldn't control other people's behavior, and that I should try to let others love me while I was learning to love myself again. I listened and began to heal. Slowly, things began to change, and it became progressively easier to ask for help. For the first time in my life I felt not alone. I realized that many other people struggle with their own demons and challenges, and this realization helped me to start facing my own.

We are fortunate to be living in a time when there is a support group for every possible need. From twelve-step programs to running clinics, professional networks to spiritual communities, adult education classes to therapy groups, there is much to choose from. Take advantage of this. Do some research, talk to the people involved, ask a lot of questions. Then get involved with a group. Getting involved with a group of people who have come from a similar place and who can show you from their own experience how to find your way can be incredibly life-affirming. And until you find your own way, the group can buoy you and support you through anything.

Reach out to family members and close friends, and gather their support as you embark on this journey. Open yourself up to the people who already love and know you. Share your fears, your hopes, your dreams, your confusions with those you trust. Reach out and then listen to what they have to say. Listening to others talk about their lives, passions, and problems and in turn talking about your own to others, whether loved ones or strangers, will help bring clarity and direction to your thinking. As you listen, you will put aside your own problems for a while and gain perspective on them. And as you realize that everyone struggles with problems, you will feel less alone.

If you haven't a clue what you want to do or what direction you want to take, you will soon know. If you know where you'd like to go but feel stuck, you will become unstuck. Allowing others to help you with your process will bring many rewards. Simply by reaching out to others you will build self-awareness. You will gain a perspective on yourself and your life that you never had before. You will learn to listen in new ways. You will begin to understand the paradox that even though in the end we are all completely and utterly alone, we can't possibly get there without some help from others.

⑥ YOU ARE NOT DOING THIS ALONE

When I was a child I happily went to church and Sunday School every week, said my prayers nightly, and had many conversations with my friends about God as we tried to grasp the idea that God was not born, He just was; a concept I now define as beginningless beginning and endless end. Without coming to any conscious understanding, we all simply relied on faith that God was good and that He was looking after us all the time. Slowly, as I saw that the world didn't conform to my idea of what was right and good, I began to distrust God. Eventually, I ditched God once and for all. I decided that He was unreliable and could not be counted on. I was not getting what I wanted, when I wanted it. I lived for many years thinking that I had no God in my life. Yet I would admit to having a guardian angel, since something was saving me from complete dissolution. I have since learned that while I may have ditched God, God had not ditched me. I was being cared for by something or someone outside myself.

When I again allowed myself to trust other people, I began to hear from many whom I most trusted and respected that a belief in God, or some greater being or power, was necessary to truly live in serenity. I was told that I could no longer rely only on myself and my ego. I wasn't ready to return to the God of my childhood, and I wasn't looking for complete serenity, which I thought sounded boring, but I also could not completely discount what I was hearing. I could not risk returning to my previous way of life. So I began to consider the possibility that some power other than my own was in charge of my life. Just being open to this possibility created a shift inside me so dramatic that everything began to change. The internal meltdown that was sparked by this sliver of willingness was miraculous. The self- and other-awareness that bloomed from this openness was remarkable. I was initially unaware of this change until other people started pointing it out to me. It actually manifested itself outwardly. I became softer, less hard-edged, easier to be around. And at some point I was aware that the black ball of fear that dwelled in my heart was cracking and slowly evaporating. This convinced me that I was not working alone, that some other force was assisting me. In the past, no matter how hard I tried to will away my fear and dissipate the despair lodged in my heart, nothing I did on my own worked.

Once we begin to admit to ourselves that we cannot live happily in isolation, once we begin to reach out to others, and once we open our hearts and minds to the possibility of God, then we can transform our lives, diminish our troubles, and increase our opportunities. The word *God* is used here to encompass all varieties of God, not just the traditional one; though if that is your idea of God then by all means use it. But some of us may need to look elsewhere. *God* can mean higher power or universal creator, collective unconscious or the universe itself, the underlying unity of all matter or our higher self. What we want to get to is the belief that something bigger and more powerful is working in this world than each, separated, one of us. When we recognize this other power, our world just naturally becomes bigger and friendlier. When we open up to a force that's greater than ourselves, we lose much of our fear. And when our fears subside, our inner voice becomes more accessible.

Write about your understanding of and your relationship with God, even if such a relationship does not yet exist. What do you expect from this relationship? Does this God have shape, color, meaning? How does it play in your life? What about it would you like to change? If you resist this whole concept, then write about that. Be willing to look at your fear. Above all, be honest with yourself. What is your equivalent of my black ball of fear? Write about that, your relationship to it, how it is serving your purpose right now, or where you'd like it to go. Take your time with this exercise, breathe as you go along, and trust that the truth will reveal itself if you make this effort.

I believe that desperation is a great motivator and that most spiritual pursuits are fueled by desperate conditions and situations. Crisis often brings out the best in people. For the duration of the crisis we put aside our petty problems and focus on the matter at hand. Time and time again I see this simple theory in practice as communities come together after natural disasters, participating in a joint effort to rebuild their lives. Witness the behavior of the people in Atlanta after the bomb explosion during the summer 1996 Olympics. People at the site who weren't hurt stayed to help those who were rather than running in fear and thinking only of themselves. In such cases, people seem to step outside themselves, outside their self-centered lives, and begin to care deeply about the world around them and the welfare of others. Chances are, their view of the world permanently shifts. Awareness is piqued, and they no longer exist only for themselves. Their true self is heard and rises to the occasion.

Did you ever spend extended time in bed as a child with chicken pox, measles, a broken limb, or something more serious? Such a forced withdrawal from the world can be an opportunity to see the world from a new angle. If it happens when we're very young, we may not already have a fixed or rigid outlook on life. Such experiences are often the most vivid for us, the ones we most cherish from our bag of memories. Something happens during these times that shifts our perspective on our small world, though we probably can't quite articulate it yet. We may even have trouble understanding it now. We experienced pain, our normal world was turned upside down, and we had to adjust ourselves to the circumstances and not focus on what we were missing. We had to take advantage of the possibilities in this new situation. As adults, catastrophic experiences such as a heart attack, loss of a job, or the break-up of a relationship can send us spinning into fear and self-pity. But how many people do you know who have used such occasions as opportunities to reevaluate their lives and priorities? Calamitous events can shock us into seeing things differently. Pleasant events and achievements can also serve to shift our awareness, but it has been my personal experience (and that of many others) that the painful events are the most powerful in opening our eyes.

While each of us can become complacent in our life, waking to the bigger world only with a catastrophic shock, it is not necessary to wait for such an event before we seek to transform our lives. We can make some progress along this road before we are faced with a disaster, as is inevitable. And once we take this road, normal life events such as illness and death will no longer be seen as disastrous but will be taken in stride, even with the pain.

As we grow up we develop and nurture our own specific view of the world. This view is influenced by our families, our neighbors, our experiences, and our own self-nature. We might, as we mature, learn by our so-called mistakes. Perhaps with each little hurt experienced along the way we learn to avoid certain situations or people. Maybe we steel our hearts against further pain, until our world gets smaller and smaller and our hearts and minds get tighter and more fearful. We see things our way and are too afraid to entertain or even allow other views. This may sound extreme, and maybe you even pride yourself on your open mind. Congratulations. Then you are ready for this. But I think that most of us, if we are truly honest with ourselves, have some degree of fear, especially when it comes to change.

All it takes to learn to see again is an open mind, an open heart, self-honesty, and humility. As you learn to see your world in a new light, more than just your vision will change. All your senses will be touched and eventually transformed by these new awarenesses. As your world gets shaken up, you will begin to hear things differently. The voices from without and within will register as they never have before. You will begin to hear the truth of your inner self. At first you may not even recognize it, but if you listen long and hard enough you will begin to become aware of it. So. Open your eyes. Open your ears. Open your heart. And you will be fine.

GOD IS IN THE DETAILS

If you take the suggestions outlined here, you will begin to notice your awareness blossom. As you open to your world, start paying attention to the details around you. One small thing you can do to constantly remind yourself to stay alert, to keep your eyes open, to look for the miracles in your everyday life, is to move your watch to your opposite wrist. Seems like such a small thing. No problem, you might say. Just try it. You might be surprised by the consequences. First, you may have a hard time even strapping it to the other wrist. Right side up gets all turned around. You will probably continue to look at the usual wrist each time you want to know the time and may even be bothered by the feel of the watch around the other wrist. It may feel awkward at first. That is just the feeling we're looking for. When you wear your watch on its usual wrist, the watch disappears; you are hardly aware of its presence. When it is placed on your other wrist, your awareness of the watch is heightened, and you might even experience discomfort.

Notice how many times each day you automatically check your wrist for the time. Each time you do so and register an awkward feeling, remind yourself to look around. Notice where you are, whom you're with, the color of the table in front of you, your friend's hairstyle or new shirt. Utilize your purpose tool—breathe and ground yourself in the now.

Einstein once said that God is in the details. Keep this in mind as you move through your life with your new eyes. If you had to, could you give an accurate description of the man who serves you coffee each morning, or of the newspaper vendor? What color are your boss's eyes?

For one week, as you begin to pay attention to the details around you, at the end of each day write in your *Quiet Corner* notebook as much of the day's details as you can remember. Be specific. If you noticed a window box with flowers, name the flowers and their colors. Pansies, gold and purple. Choose your own style to record your recollections. Write in narrative form, or write a poem. Tell a story, or make a list. The form doesn't matter, just the details. You may want to jot things down throughout the day. Make a habit of carrying around a small notebook for just such occasions.

Move your watch, change your life.

As we progress through our lives and construct layer upon layer of protection, our true self may get buried and lost to us, if only partially. No wonder we have trouble getting to it—we've crushed it beneath the defenses we learn that help us maneuver our way through the world. Rather than thinking of yourself as a demon, think of yourself as an overprotective parent. Your child, or inner voice, is deep within you suffocating from all the protective clothing you draped on it for its own good. It is up to you to uncover it and allow it to breathe. Here is a simple exercise that will help you relax and get out of your head and into your body.

Lie on the floor with your hands at your sides, palms up. Close your eyes and relax your whole body, beginning with your toes. Take your time with this exercise. Spend at least ten or fifteen minutes each time you do it. Breathe into your toes and feet, stretching, flexing, then relaxing. Once relaxed, forget about them. Move up your leg with your breath. Stretch, relax, and then forget about your shins, your calves, your knees, your thighs. Continue up your whole body, slowly, concentrating on each part of your body, bringing every ounce of your attention with you, with your breath, as you move up. Stretch, relax, and then forget about each small section. Remember to breathe as you go along. Move up slowly to the crown of your head until all is relaxed. You might put on some soft, soothing music, light some candles, turn out the lights. Pay attention to your breath. Use it to relax you. When you are completely relaxed, put your breath into your tummy, relax your stomach, and just breathe. Fill your tummy with air on the inhale, deflate it on the exhale. Softly, naturally.

Now try to visualize where your inner voice is located and how much protection surrounds it. Gradually strip away the layers to expose your center. This will take some practice. Freeing your voice will not be immediate. The purpose of this exercise right now is just to bring your attention to your inner self via your breath. No need to do anything else. As you repeat and continue this exercise, your awareness will increase. And that is all we're looking for here—heightened awareness. Be loving and gentle with yourself as you do this. Invite your higher power to be your guide and you will learn to see as you once saw. It's okay to be afraid and to feel silly, it's natural. So continue to trust in the process. Breathe and become more aware with each breath.

3

Letting Go

WILLINGNESS

Do you always need to be right? Do you need to have the last word in any verbal exchange, especially if it's an argument? Do you ever think: "If only people would behave the way I want them to, everything would be fine. We'd all get along, there'd be no reason to quarrel"? If so, I'd venture to say that you're not alone. Many of us think we know the solution to other people's problems, even if they are not aware that they have a problem. Some of us are rude and overbearing, while others are overly gracious and sweet, as we try to impose our will and outlook onto others. Our intentions may be good, yet we may be causing harm without knowing it.

It is always easier to look at someone else's life and know what needs fixing than to get close enough to our own to identify a problem. We only need look at our intimate love relationships to understand this phenomenon. How many times have friends given you advice on your love life while their own was crumbling before their eyes unbeknownst to them? Or vice versa? Why do people remain in relationships that for all the world appear unhealthy and unsafe? Why do we lose sight of ourselves so easily and have such clarity when looking at others?

Most of us are taught that too much time spent on ourselves is narcissistic and selfish, so we learn to focus on others. In the process, we lose touch with ourselves and feel guilty or shameful each time we turn inward. But we cannot get to our own true voice unless we turn toward ourselves, which can be a frightening prospect. Perhaps we are afraid of what we'll find; maybe our deepest fears about ourselves will be revealed. Or if we look there might be nothing at all there. Where do these fears come from? If we take a minute to look back at our childhood, we discover that none of this fear was present when we were young. We were not self-conscious, we had no need to control ourselves or others; we simply lived with ourselves, comfortable in our own skin. The fear came later, as we ventured into the world by ourselves. This fear then incited our desire to control all that came our way. Dealing with the unknown was too risky, because we thought we were never given the tools we needed to face it.

For the time being, I invite you and give you permission to focus on yourself for a while, to return to your child-nature. Turn your sight inward as you search for and explore the real you. Trust that you have all the inner resources necessary to confront the unknown. Trust me when I say that if you do this, by the time you are ready to again turn your focus to others you will be more loving, patient, and understanding. And your need to control the world around you will be much diminished.

All you need is the willingness to look, an open mind to approach what you see, and the courage to move forward. In this process, as you begin to relinquish control over others, you will also need to relinquish control over yourself. So for now, try to move through your life as a passenger. Get out of the driver's seat. And simply enjoy the view.

As you move toward uncovering your true voice, there will be many opportunities to begin the practice of letting go and nurturing your willingness. It all begins with awareness. If you are not aware of your behavior, there's no hope in changing it. So try each day to hone your awareness and, by extension, practice being willing.

For one week, at the end of each day sit down with your notebook and pen and recall some of the events of the day. Did you have an argument with anyone? Even if you were right, did you keep insisting self-righteously, determined to sway the other person? Were you ever annoyed about slow-moving traffic or a slow waiter? Or by people moving too fast? Why? Can you see how the movement of others is out of your control? Can you see how your annoyance helped nothing?

Don't use this exercise as a reason to beat yourself up. You are not perfect, you are doing the best you can for the moment, and you are practicing willingness. As your willingness grows, so will your awareness. You will begin to see how much your focus is turned outward, how you avoid being alone with yourself, how easily distracted you get by your surroundings. Don't attempt to change anything yet. Be gentle with yourself. Just look with your new eyes, be aware of your actions, and continue to be willing to move through whatever discomfort this may cause as you reach into yourself and grow into your true being. Consider the discomfort growing pains as you stretch your mind and heart to fit their new and rightful place in your life.

TAKE THE COTTON OUT OF YOUR EARS AND PUT IT IN YOUR MOUTH

If we want to hone our listening skills so we can hear our inner voice, we must also learn to listen to the outer world. If we are not good listeners, we will never learn to hear the truth of ourselves.

It takes a very long time to develop our listening skills and to learn to truly hear what is being said to us—both from within and from without. Even once we acquire these skills, we must continue to hone them and never take them for granted. Early along on this path, when other people talk to you and try to share their experience with you, you might begin to use the two words that became my favorites: "I know." When we use these words it probably means that we're not really listening. Or we hear what we want to hear. Maybe we believe we're too old not to know or to admit that we don't know. Maybe we need to know things even before we actually know them. This lesson is often taught to us as children, and some of us learn it very well—so well, in fact, that it becomes hard to unlearn.

My good friend Barbara helped me with this one day when she brought my attention to my "I know" reflexive response behavior. I was seeking her advice on how to handle a difficult relationship that was falling apart. I kept initiating contact with this person, which always ended up making me miserable. Then I would call Barbara and ask her what I should do. She would, of course, tell me to stay away from him, to instead spend time with people who truly loved me, to pay attention to my spiritual well-being, and to pray for guidance. I would say, "I know, I know," and then go on to talk more about him—how he hurt me, why didn't he love me, how I was the right woman for him, and when would he see that. I continued to seek out this man, and I continued to get hurt. I continued to call Barbara and cry on her shoulder. I wanted her to tell me that things would change, that he would come back to me, that I was doing the right things. She didn't say any of this, and even though I was frustrating her she kept giving me good advice. I kept saying "I know" without really listening.

Perhaps we repeat "I know" almost as a mantra when we're first learning how to listen, because deep inside maybe we do know and upon hearing the truth from someone else we recognize it as the truth. But I wasn't letting Barbara know that I heard her and appreciated her help, nor was I implementing any of her suggestions in my life. One day she suggested that I take the cotton out of my ears and put it in my mouth. In other words, she told me to shut up and listen. At first I was offended, but I had grown to trust Barbara and so took the suggestion. I didn't do it always or perfectly, but slowly my ears began to unclog and my life began to change even more. I learned to keep my mouth shut even if I thought, "I know, I know already."

If we aren't busy talking, we can hear better. If we aren't busy trying to figure out the answer, we can learn more. If we stop trying to manipulate or twist the truth, we will begin to shed our delusions. If we stop attempting to fill the silences that are normal in any conversation, we can begin to appreciate the silence and its message. If we are quiet enough, we will be better able to hear.

Letting go is probably the most difficult concept to grasp and the most challenging action to perform on the *Quiet Corner* path. Yet without this in our repertoire, all else is for naught. I continue to learn valuable lessons about myself and my world according to both the ease with which I am able to let go and the tenacity I exhibit as I cling desperately to something, unwilling to release my hold, however tentative.

My first glimmer of understanding about what it means to let go came while I was in the back seat of a New York City taxicab. A friend and I were on our way to meet a group of people to see a Broadway play. We had plenty of time to get to the theater fifteen minutes before curtain time and decided to splurge on a cab rather than take a subway or bus. We flagged down a cab and relaxed in the back seat for the fifteen-minute trip. About ten or fifteen minutes later I became aware that we were neither moving nor sitting at a traffic light. We had twenty blocks to go. Looking at my watch, I noticed we had five minutes to meet our friends and twenty to make it on time for the start of the play. I immediately began to worry.

I sat on the edge of the seat. I assessed the traffic. I constantly referred to the time and noticed it slipping away—faster than usual, it seemed. I talked to the driver, asked him what he planned to do to get us to our destination on time. I fretted. I twitched. I watched.

My friend was much calmer than I, sitting back in his seat looking quite relaxed. Traffic wasn't moving, our friends were waiting, show time was now only ten minutes away—how could he sit there and do nothing? He then suggested that I join him and just relax. We couldn't move the traffic any faster than it was moving, sitting on the edge of the seat in an anxious state accomplished nothing, our friends would understand if we were late, chances were the play wouldn't start exactly on time anyway, and we were moving, however slowly, so we'd get there eventually. Why not let go and just relax? I laughed, exhaled, and just let go, slouching down in the seat. We got to the theater on time, and I was never so relieved to be someplace. It has been at least ten years since that cab ride, and I don't think I'll ever forget it. I use it as a reminder each time I notice that I am trying to control the uncontrollable.

People seem to magically appear in our lives when we need to learn a spiritual lesson. If we are open and willing and able to listen, we will find that our lives are filled with these spiritual teachers. When we first learn about letting go and are told by one of these spiritual teachers that we are not in charge of things, that there is a force greater and more powerful than we at work in our lives, we might think that we then have to do nothing. Give up control, let the universe do its thing, and just sit back, not participate in life, and wait to die. Or we might believe that being in our life means being in charge. We don't know how to just be. But gradually we learn that being in our life and turning the reigns over to a force much greater does not mean being in a static, dull life. We become more active than ever, more fully alive and in our life than ever before.

One important lesson about letting go is that the greater our fear, the more we cling. The less fearful we are, the easier it is to let go. When we can let go, even as we sit in fear, miracles happen.

The 1996 gold medalist in women's platform diving was said to have no fear as she stood ten meters above the water preparing for each dive. Her composure was rock solid, her dives were graceful, and she deserved the gold medal. Her competitors were skilled Olympic divers also capable of winning the gold. I believe that the winner showed up prepared and well trained like everyone else. What stood her apart from the rest was her lack of fear.

Without fear, she was free to simply concentrate on her technique. I admired this in her, but even more so I admired the other divers' ability to climb to the top of the platform *with* their fear and dive the ten meters anyway. Years of training on each dive couldn't eliminate their fear. Each of them deserves a gold medal. So take their example—don't wait for the fear to leave before letting go. Just dive.

Show up, train, participate, learn the skills necessary to compete, and then just let go and trust. If we can do this each day of our lives, then we will all win the gold. Allow the divine to enter your life. If we hold on in fear, clinging to our achievements and desires, then grace will not have an opportunity to visit. If we sit in fear, our hearts and minds will become clouded and our true voice will get pushed deeper and deeper. So free your voice by letting go. And letting go. And letting go.

JUST THE FACTS

For one week, observe your behavior and try to be aware of times when you are anxious or fearful. Each night, record in your *Quiet Corner* notebook unpleasant encounters you had with other people or simply the unpleasant feeling you walked away with. Become your own private, personal life reporter. Just write the facts. Don't judge. Don't even try to change. Just try to heighten your awareness.

The next week, notice these events as they're happening and practice letting go, right there and then. Not forever. Just one incident at a time. When arguing with a friend, let go of the need to be right, even if you are right. Let go of the desire to help someone who resists it. Let go of the delusion that by simply willing it you can change the flow of traffic. Write about these experiences. How easy or hard was it to let go? Were you successful each time you made the attempt? Record your struggle, your feelings, your awareness.

Let go, let go, let go. And let the universe carry on for a while without your help. At the end of the week, review what happened or didn't. How different were your feelings the second week versus the first? Write it all down. This is important stuff. It may not be learning the way you're used to, but it's learning nonetheless—about what truly makes you tick and how you can let go and invite grace into your life and give expression to your inner truth.

Whether we live in a bustling metropolis, a crowded suburb, or a sleepy rural area, most of us are always and utterly busy with things to do, places to go, people to see. And there's never enough time to do it all. Feed the kids, walk the dog, visit your mother, please the boss. And even if you have help, the responsibilities of it all seem to fall on your shoulders, and you feel like you're doing it all even if you're not. Pay the bills, water the plants, research colleges, visit the accountant, keep in touch with friends. Stress and anxiety build up to overwhelm you; even small decisions seem monumental and become difficult to make. What to wear to work. Where to eat lunch. What to buy Dad for his birthday. The stress that results from such overload affects all areas of our lives—our performance at work, our relationships with friends and lovers, our self-esteem, the way we treat our pets. The least little thing can cause us to "lose it" and then engage in regrettable behavior or say things we don't mean. Sound familiar? We have all done this at one point or another. Following the *Quiet Corner* path you will learn how to lessen your stress, manage your life, and deal with whatever comes your way.

Even if we've learned to let go, even if we've made time to sit and breathe, even if we've talked to several people about our plight, sometimes nothing seems to work. It's all just too much. Sometimes we truly want to disappear. We don't care about finding our voice. We just want to be someone else with a different life.

The good news is that this is all quite normal, and there is a creative solution that will cause no harm. Although a temporary fix, it is critical to carry with you in your new *Quiet Corner* box of tools. You can simplify your life immediately by taking just one issue that presently gnaws at you and putting it aside. Tell yourself to simply "put it on the shelf." Imagine a shelf in your *Quiet*

Corner built for the explicit purpose of holding all those things that you can't quite contain for the moment. All those things that are spilling over from your head and heart, things that are creating stress and undue anxiety in your life.

Start by relieving yourself of issues that are furthest away. The visit you are planning to your in-laws next month. There's too much emotional strain in their home right now, or you just don't get along—the last thing you need with all that's happening in your own home is to spend time with them. Keep the plan, but put it on the shelf. You don't have to decide today whether you should go. Deal with it next week. Then, the meeting scheduled with your boss tomorrow. You're prepared, ready for it, so put it on the shelf until tomorrow. You will be there soon enough, no need to worry about what might transpire. Continue to sort through the confusion and clear stuff away so that you have some breathing room. Even the decision you're struggling with about returning to school next year. Put that on the shelf. Remember, you're not discarding any of these things or even forgetting about them. For that matter, you're not even putting them out of sight. You're just putting them on your *Quiet Corner* shelf. They are there, ready and waiting for you when you are ready for them.

And even if you don't return on your own to the things you've put on your shelf, you will be reminded of them when they fall off and hit you in the head, when it's time to face them again. Putting things on the shelf is not to deny their existence, it's just to clear away the space they take up in your mind and heart, keeping you from hearing your deep inner truth. So move them out of the way. Spend time on your inner journey. And deal with them one at a time when the time is right.

PRACTICE

Right now, as you read this, experiment with putting something on your shelf, even if you're not particularly overwhelmed at the moment. It will be good practice, honing this new tool. Close your eyes and quickly sort through the issues that are uppermost in your mind, the chores that need doing, the decisions that must be made. Now imagine that shelf. What does it look like? What is it made of? Its color? How high is it? Now select one of the big issues from the scan you just did and place it on the shelf. Now choose something else, something smaller—the laundry per-haps—and place it on the shelf also. Keep your eyes closed for a few more moments. Breathe. Take three deep breaths and focus on that. In your mind, walk away from the shelf, knowing where it is and how to get back to it, and return to your life. Now open your eyes. How do you feel? Are you okay about those two items being left on the shelf? Can you keep them there for a day? Go back and retrieve them tomorrow?

Now take out your notebook and write about the experience. Write about what you chose to put there. Then think about why you chose what you did. Could be there's no attachment to what you chose. That's okay. Think about the things that came up that you were unwilling to put away, that you wanted to hang on to. This is your experience. It is your shelf. Your choices, your expe-rience, will be unlike any other. Savor it. Learn from it. Keep doing it. You might even want to build or designate a real shelf in your *Quiet Corner* rather than just imagine one. Some day, if you continue to follow the *Quiet Corner* path, you will no longer need such a shelf. Everything in your heart and mind at any given moment will be manageable. And that's a promise!

TAKE A BATH

As you experiment with and learn to use your new "put it on the shelf" tool, take note of the behavior you used prior to this when you were in the overwhelm mode. How did you relieve the pressure? Did you escape to another dimension using real or imagined substances? Are you still engaging in such behavior? Write about this. Has putting things on the shelf helped curb the old behavior? Are you now aware that the cigarette, the extra piece of cake, the excessive exercising, or the fantasizing might be your way of coping with being overwhelmed? I'm not asking you to stop all such behavior now. Just use your new tool and be aware, be aware, be aware. And treat yourself to an extra long bubble bath or double feature. You deserve it.

TIME

Time is money. Time is all we have. There's never enough of it. We always want more. Time heals. Time flies. Time waits for no one. Time is on our side.

Whatever we think or feel about time, it usually enters the equation of our daily lives in some measure. Usually, there's not enough of it. But we set priorities in our lives, and not having enough time is never a good reason not to do something—it's only an excuse. Yet it's easy to use this reason to keep us away from the *Quiet Corner* path, especially if we convince ourselves that all this sitting still and writing about ourselves is a luxury, a waste of time.

Being on this path is not a luxury unless you believe that living a full, rich, contented life is a luxury. It's not. And once you make some progress on this path you'll understand this. It becomes a necessity, and therefore you find the time. But in the beginning, before you receive the fruits of this practice, time can keep you away.

Recently, I met a woman at a weekend writing conference who desperately wants to write. She has five children ages four to fourteen, so she certainly has her hands full. But she wants to write. And she knows that if she does she'll like herself and her life more. But she can't figure out how she's going to find the time to write. It was suggested that she find one hour a week to write. She knew she could do that—just one hour a week. Maybe she was expecting that to write she'd have to find ten or fifteen or even twenty hours a week. Impossible. One hour she could do. Two pages a week. One hundred pages a year. That she could do.

If time is an issue for you, you can probably find one hour a week to get started. That is enough for now. As you proceed, you'll find more of it. If you want this badly enough, if you want anything badly enough, you'll find the time.

⑥ IS THERE A GOD IN YOUR LIFE?

Here we are at perhaps the trickiest part of the road and the one most fraught with potholes. Just as there are myriad attitudes and opinions on this planet, there are different religious views, many different faces of God (or none at all). Your personal beliefs on this matter need not be swayed to follow this path. Just keep an open mind and trust that your beliefs will fit into the *Quiet Corner* framework. I've seen people get to this juncture in the road and use their belief or nonbelief as an excuse to not move forward. Think twice or even three or four times before you make that decision. It could mean the difference between a thriving, spiritually connected life and one bogged down in self-righteousness. The matters we will be discussing are spiritual, not religious, ones. So bring along your views on religion, if you like, as we all learn to make a spiritual connection to ourselves and our world.

Individuality, self-motivation, entrepreneurship—these are all familiar states that we strive to achieve. Nothing wrong here. But too often, especially if we are successful in our endeavors, we tend to believe that we are alone, that our achievements have all been a result of our own hard work, and nothing else. Some of this is certainly true, but wouldn't this mean that your failures and misfortunes are also due to you? Funny how we can so easily take credit for the "good" stuff and throw blame for the "bad." It's human nature, we all do it. But just as no one else is completely responsible for your personal tragedies, neither are you completely responsible for the triumphs.

I'd like to introduce the idea of referring to all these things— "good" and "bad"—as gifts, given to us in this life to move us forward through the human experience, to teach us about what it means to be human, and to reward us for our authentic enthusiasm and willingness. We will talk more about good and bad and right and wrong later on. For now, try not to label anything in your life as good or bad, right or wrong. Just experience it all without labeling. And then trust that all these things are being given to you by a force that's operating in your life. Even if you decide to do nothing, your life will still happen. It is much more pleasant, however, if you participate in your own life. Besides, doing nothing is actually a form of participating anyway, so you can't not participate even if you want to.

Now close your eyes and imagine what this force in your life looks like. Is it God as you know Him or Her? Is it an invisible force in the universe? Is it your good or bad upbringing? If you have trouble visualizing something concrete, that's okay too. Perhaps you can imagine it as the wind. Strong, assertive, unpredictable, unknowable, gentle. Now decide, since it is there anyway, that you will let this force take care of you, you will let it do its job. This alone will free you of the weight you might sometimes put on your shoulders. Let this force take it. It can handle it.

At any given moment during the day, check in with yourself and notice your relationship with this force. Who is dominant— you or it? If you're feeling stressed, incapable of movement or even thought, consult with this grace and let it take over. Ask for guidance. It is there to help. And it will. If your image of this force shifts and changes even throughout the course of one day, that's okay, let it.

Little by little, as you grow accustomed to having this force in your life and trusting it to take care of you, you will give more and more of your life to it. You will then be available to spend your emotional energy on heightening your awareness, on finding your voice, and on really getting to the truth of you. There's no need to tread this path alone. Give yourself a break and let grace guide you. It will be the strongest partnership you ever forge.

HUMILITY

As you learn about this force in your life and its relationship to you, and as your commitment to this *Quiet Corner* path deepens, begin to commune with this power each day. For one week, practice the following:

As soon as you wake up each morning, roll off your bed onto your knees and greet the day in this humble posture. Ask grace to guide you throughout the day. And before you retire each day, assume this same posture by the side of your bed and give thanks to this higher power for guiding you through another day. Even if you don't have a clear idea of this power, do this anyway. If you are too embarrassed to kneel by your bed, do it elsewhere, or do it on top of the bed. But do it. If you are not used to praying or if even the idea of it causes you consternation, let that go and just do it. Praying is a form of letting go and will give you daily practice in this most necessary of *Quiet Corner* skills. Do it for one week. Then stop doing it for one week. Then try another week of doing it. Take notes. Observe your life. Do you feel any different from week to week? All you're doing here is becoming aware that left solely to yourself you cannot gracefully run your own life. That all you need is an open mind, a willing attitude, and a dose of humility to ask for help. And that help is there if you want it. So ask and you shall receive.

BREATH AS MIRACLE

If you are having trouble with the concept of God or a higher force, don't be discouraged. Maybe you've had to make your way in this world by yourself. Maybe you feel that if something needs doing no one can do it as well as you. Maybe you've given your heart over many times only to be given it back hurt and in sorrow, so you've stopped the practice. Maybe you just don't believe that anything, including an invisible force, can help you and that you are in charge of your life—there is nothing you cannot handle. Well, I understand. And you are probably not the only one out there who feels the way you do. You are not as unique in this as you think. But before you turn your back, try this first:

Close your eyes and bring your attention to your breath. Where is your breath? Is it in your throat or deep in your belly? Can you bring it down into your belly if it isn't already there? Since you're in control here, of course you can. Keep paying attention to your breath and how you can control it. Breathe deeply. Breathe shallowly. Breathe into your back, your neck, your head. Now relax again and just breathe naturally for a few moments. Don't force your breath. Just let it go where it goes. Now try to hold your breath. Will your breathing to stop. When you sputter back into your life, consider what brought your breath back to you if you yourself were intent on holding it. Did you decide to start breathing again, or did your breath decide? Where does your breath come from? Can you perhaps see your breath as a miracle of life? If so, consider this as a force bigger and greater than you alone. Consider this as something to refer to when your ego insists that you are alone and independent, relying on nothing else. You have your breath. Your breath has you. Accept this miracle and give yourself a break. Be grateful for each breath and admit it as a gift. While reading this book, use the words *My Breath* whenever I use the words *God* or *Higher Power*. Don't get bogged down in semantics. Your breath is yours and can guide you through this as well as someone else's God can guide them. So come along, breathe, and define your "God/Breath" however you wish.

⑥ TURNING IT OVER AND OVER AND OVER AGAIN

We would all like our lives and the lives of those we love to be productive, fruitful, and happy. We probably have a scenario in our minds of what constitutes a "perfect" life. And since we have this already fully constructed and contrived life in our minds, we might experience frustration and even disappointment each time something happens or doesn't happen to fit in with our plan. We may not call it a plan and we may not consciously know the full extent of it, but each time we experience disappointment or frustration with the workings of the world, it probably means that we've had an expectation of sorts. Even minor frustrated expectations can cause grief and emotional setbacks. And this has the potential to blind us to the gifts being offered to us by the universe that we hadn't the power or inclination to envision on our own.

In 1991 when I lost my job and my boyfriend at the same time, I was holding on so tightly to both of these things that I was devastated when they were ripped away. They had helped me create an image of myself that I projected into the world. I now see those losses as gifts. I never would have chosen them for myself, but today my life is fuller and richer as a result. I was able to turn my life over and trust that I would be okay. Trust that if I just let go and followed my heart rather than my fear only the best would follow, even if I could not envision at the time what that was.

So practice turning things over. And here comes the rub. Practice without expectations! Once we have an expectation, we only set ourselves up for disappointment. So try to turn things over and let them go without looking for the gift that was promised there. If you look for it, you'll give it a shape or meaning or color. If you don't, then you can be truly surprised. Practice first on the small stuff. If you expect people to show up early for appointments because that is your habit, simply let go of that and turn it over. If you experience disappointment when someone cancels a date at the last minute, even if they have a legitimate reason, let it go and turn it over. Let it go and don't expect things to go the way you want them to, when you want them to. Realize that you cannot control the behavior of others. Turn it over. Without letting go and turning it over, your attitude makes it hard to enjoy the company of someone who arrives late or the unexpected free time in your schedule that a cancellation opens up.

Do you expect loved ones to read your mind and give you exactly what you want for your birthday or Valentine's Day? You might have this expectation because you've dropped enough hints and they should know you well enough to get it right. To avoid the disappointment that this expectation sets up, first you could communicate clearly what you would like and, second, turn it over and allow this person to make their own choice. Let it go, turn it over, and be surprised and happy with whatever comes, with however love is expressed to you, even if it's not how you would choose to express it.

Practice on the small stuff, and then move on to the bigger issues as you gain experience. This is an acquired skill, and it takes lots of practice to become good at it. I'm not sure it's something we ever completely master, so be patient with yourself. Are you expecting a raise? Aside from doing your best on the job and communicating to your superiors what you would like from them, you cannot determine the amount before you know it. And it would be unwise to spend it before you get it. So after doing all you can, let it go, turn it over, and trust that it will come—in the right time and in the right amount. Afraid of an encounter next week, with your dentist, boyfriend, boss, mother? Is your mind imagining what will be said, done, or felt? Remember that you are not there yet and you cannot tell the future, so prepare yourself as well as you can—physically, emotionally, mentally—and then just let it go, show up on time, and turn it over again as you meet and throughout the entire session. Each time you feel a wave of anxiety or fear, turn it over, let it go.

Do this letting go and turning things over exercise for a week. Don't make anything too important. Be prepared, show up, and turn it over. Remember, you are not in charge of the outcome. While there will be some situations where you may be able to accurately predict the outcome, for many, no matter how hard you impose your will, your will may not win. So to avoid disappointment, turn it over, and be ready to receive the gifts of the universe. By doing this, you won't be weighed down by your expectations and disappointments. Your inner voice will have more space in which to flower. Turn it over. Let it go. Become aware.

⑥ MAKING DECISIONS

Does everyone seem to have an opinion about your hairstyle each time you get a new cut or color? Do these comments ever determine how you feel about yourself or the decision you make the next time you visit the salon or barber shop? Have you ever made a decision based on the advice of others that has never sat comfortably with you and has perhaps come around to haunt you? Have you ever done something against your better judgment because you considered it to be expected of you or because it coincided with the majority opinion? Do you ever worry over a decision, look at all the angles, finally make the best-informed decision, one that you are satisfied with, only to question it later when new evidence comes to light or even when someone throws off a seemingly unrelated comment?

From what to eat for dinner, to where to send the kids to college, to when and where to take your next vacation, to how to deal with your aging parents—never does a day go by that does not hold opportunities to exercise the skill of making decisions. And yet no matter how many decisions we make or how easily we make them, there are those that never get made, or those that we unduly agonize over, or those that are too hastily made, causing us to suffer unforeseen consequences and spend more time than we have cleaning up after them.

Does any of this sound familiar? Do you have some issues that you can't seem to get a firm grasp on, let alone make a decision about? Chances are you've probably already thought your way through all the various scenarios leading to and beyond any decision you might make. So for the time being, stop thinking about it. Trust that you will not get to the answer by just thinking. You already have the answer to your dilemma inside you. Now all you have to do is get to it, and thinking is not the tool to use.

First, it is important to get it out of your head, so write it down. Write about the dilemma that you are currently struggling with. Should you go away for the weekend and cancel your other plans? Which job offer should you accept? Whom should you hire to care for the children? This act of writing will introduce some perspective. Try it, right now, with anything you've got on your plate. Write down the pros and cons. Don't think. Don't analyze. Don't judge. Just write.

Now close your notebook and your eyes and just breathe. Bring your attention to your breath and away from your decision. If your thoughts float back to the issue at hand, just let them go, and breathe. Now open your eyes and flip a coin. Heads it's yes, tails it's no. Quick. Do it. Don't think. As you register the result of the coin toss, notice your immediate, spontaneous reaction to the result. Were you relieved and happy? If so, this is your choice. Were you disappointed and sad? If so, go with the other choice. Don't think. Trust your intuitive responses. Don't worry about the pros and cons. Don't think about what others will say. Trust your instincts. You've done your homework. You've thought it through. Now trust your gut. Know also that there is no good or bad here, no right or wrong. Know also that in most cases any decision is the right decision. It is when we are in limbo, on the fence, that we do ourselves a disservice—we get stuck in the torment of our minds. And the noise only gets louder and drowns out our truth if we don't let it go.

So, as you make decisions and continue practicing the process of decision making, you can also begin to let go of your need to second guess yourself, your need to be perfect. Anytime your head fills up with confusion about what to do, make a decision to write about it, to pray about it, to move it out of your head and deeper into your body. (And I don't mean stuffing it down, ignoring it, and causing yourself stress-related health problems. This is never a solution.) Simply go through the process outlined here and the solution will present itself. If you wake up confused and irritable with a dilemma filling your brain and you do not have time to go through the steps toward an answer before you face your day, simply put it on the shelf until you can return to it. Don't carry it around with you. Turn it over and trust that you will get back to it and be shown the answer. Decide each day that you have a choice. Decide each day that you can turn anything over and that you will know the answer when you make room for it. Decide each day that putting a little distance between yourself and the pressures you face will bring clarity. Decide each day that your breath and your God will be with you and on your side as you face daily life. And if during the course of your day confusion sets in, make a decision to turn it over again. Start your day over again and again if necessary. As you do this turning over, you will become more aware of your breath, your God, your own reliable instincts, and, ultimately, yourself. So don't think. Don't decide anything. Just let go and let grace enter your life each and every day, throughout the day. And the answers will come. You will know what to do.

Letting go, turning it over, putting things on the shelf, making decisions—these may seem mind and action oriented and may seem to have nothing at all to do with getting inside to your true voice. Well, they have much to do with the process, and if you're diligent about following the suggestions here, each time you retreat to your *Quiet Corner* you will notice the difference and the impact these things have on getting to your quiet voice. Each time, you will carry in with you less mind noise, fewer distractions, and perhaps greater determination.

Retreating to your *Quiet Corner* and just breathing is key to the accomplishment of everything else suggested here. It is the cornerstone, the foundation, the life of all that we do here. When you learn to sit quietly—concentrating on your breath and letting your thoughts go—you will be better prepared for everything that comes along the way when you're not sitting still. Letting go of your thoughts will help you let go of any uncomfortable feelings that might get aroused as you move along the *Quiet Corner* path. Concentrating on your breath will prepare you for concentrating on other things that need your devoted attention. Getting in touch with your breath will bring you in closer touch with the real you. So throughout the process, if the other suggestions aren't working, just breathe. If you cannot even get close to being willing, just breathe. If you are putting pressure on yourself concerning any of this, just breathe. And when you learn to do this, you will carry it to the rest of your life and breathe your way through any difficulty, toward any goal, into all challenging situations. Your breath and your ability to concentrate on your breath will guide you in your personal relationships, help you to achieve perspective under all circumstances, relieve you of the need to try to control any outcome.

I will suggest exercises to help you learn how to concentrate on your breath. Here's one suggestion: Bring your attention to your breath by taking three deep, three-part breaths. Close your eyes when you do this. As you inhale, first fill up your lower chest, then your middle chest, then your upper chest. As you exhale, release your breath from the top down, first the upper chest, then the middle chest, then the lower chest. Three times. Breathe. Now open your eyes and breathe naturally and as deeply as you can. As you inhale, feel the air come in through your nose and fill up your lungs. As you exhale notice your lungs and belly deflate and feel the air moving out your nose. You might say to yourself: "As I breathe in I feel the air through my nose. As I breathe out I feel my belly deflate." Inhale—nose. Exhale—belly. Inhale—nose. Exhale—belly. Continue this for five minutes, slowly and mindfully.

As you inhale, now be aware of your surroundings. As you exhale, be grateful for where you are. Inhale—aware. Exhale—grateful. Inhale—aware. Exhale—grateful. Continue this for five minutes. Remember to keep your eyes open—let the light in.

Now as you inhale, notice the sounds around you—birds, car horns, wind in the trees, radio next door. As you exhale, smile into the sound. Inhale—sound. Exhale—smile. Inhale—sound. Exhale—smile. Continue for five minutes.

Now as you inhale, just inhale. As you exhale, just exhale. Inhale, exhale. Inhale, exhale. Continue for five, ten, or even thirty minutes. Just breathe.

4

Looking

Inside

TAKE AN INVENTORY

Up to this point on your *Quiet Corner* path you've (a) acknowledged your busy mind and the way it controls you, (b) learned how to slow your mind by sitting still and concentrating on your breath, and (c) been introduced to the concept of letting go and trusting that a force greater than yourself is operating in your life. This is a great start, and all the tools you've picked up so far will continue to serve you as you proceed further along the path and deeper into yourself. Once you've begun to hone these new skills, you will be ready to look closer at yourself and go deeper than you've gone before. One way to begin doing this is to take an internal inventory of what exactly is there. Not to analyze what's there, but just to look. In "Busy Mind" you identified some of the surface noise and nagging questions that were causing you daily stress and anxiety. Now we want to look at what remains after you've spent some time sitting still, observing, and letting go. The more you sit quietly alone, the quieter your mind will get. And the busy chatter that once so disturbed you will be the first to go, leaving you an opportunity to probe deeper.

When you sit and listen to yourself, observing your busy mind, you may become aware of two voices that are regular visitors: the judge and the critic. They almost always work in tandem and tell you, "You're not good enough. When will you ever learn? You can do so much better. Who do you think you are? You're a fraud and soon people will notice." Both of these voices are blaming and shaming and might have the tone of a parent or teacher. Identifying the source of these voices, which is different for each of us, might then cause you to turn the blame around. But blame and shame have no place in a spiritually fit mind. Our job here will be just to notice, identify the source if necessary, label what's in our minds, and resist the urge to blame, judge, criticize, or analyze.

Another voice that might appear regularly is that of the inquisitor, which questions every little thing you do or don't do and offers you no peace: "Couldn't you have been a little nicer? Do you think you were thorough enough on your latest project? What will the boss think? Shouldn't you try harder?" Again, we don't want to accuse the source here, even if we know it. We just want to look at what our mind contains. Perhaps some of us have a reporter or storyteller that helps balance these negative voices by taking us into fantasy land or self-denial, making things up that aren't real just so we can cope with whatever reality seems to be stalking us: "You're better than the rest of them; if only they'd put you in charge things would run smoother. You were meant for greatness." Even though we might think this voice serves us, you will learn how it only adds to your delusions.

It would be nice if we had a magic wand to clear away what doesn't belong to us, to distinguish for us the voices inside that are part of our own true essence and those that we adopted from our caretakers, our teachers, our idols, and friends. By the time we begin to take a look, it's often difficult to tell what's ours and what's been borrowed. We can't just line things up in our mind and in seconds rid our brains of the dust and the trash and the merchandise on loan—except temporarily as we learned in the "Clean Sweep Your Mind" exercise. But if we take the time, we can look inside, become familiar with what's there, and start to weed the garden of our soul. Just as with weeds, some will be easy to pull up and discard and others will be deep-rooted and tenacious, while still others will appear beautiful and convince us that they are not even weeds. Little by little, as we begin to clear things away, we will learn the differences and soon have a thriving garden filled with abundance and flowers that belong only to us.

Each time you visit your *Quiet Corner* to sit still and breathe, learn what's there inside you and what should stay and what should go. As you sit and breathe, thoughts will rise up and announce themselves. As you begin you will probably be seduced by many of these thoughts and perhaps follow them to their conclusion before you become aware that you've lost track of counting or your breath. This is very normal in the beginning and should not discourage you. Simply bring your attention back to your breath and your counting each time you notice this happening. At the end of each session, try to recall what thoughts came up. Write them down. You might encounter some anger as you go deeper into yourself. You might be angry with your mother for what she didn't give you. You might be angry at society for burdening you with gender expectations. You might be angry with your partner for not being who you thought he was. Don't let this anger trap you. Notice it, write about it. Don't analyze. Just observe it and let it go. You may have to work hard to accomplish this. It won't go away at first bidding. But each time you encounter it, let a little bit go and it will eventually fade from your mind, heart, and body.

Begin a section in your notebook called "My Inventory." As

you begin to get in touch with your innermost being, record here what you find. Don't sit each time with the intention of cataloguing whatever comes up. Sit with the intention of just sitting and breathing. You don't have to find your thoughts. They will find you. And if they never come when you sit, great. You can skip this part and move on. But if they do come, just observe, let them go, keep breathing. Later, when your session has ended, write down what you remember. Be specific. Don't judge. Become aware. And go deep.

OBSERVE, DON'T ANALYZE, BE HONEST

As things begin to rise up to inform you about yourself and all that's inside, as you do your self-inventory, and as you take notice of your busy mind, you may be inclined to want to analyze what you discover. The why and how of things might begin to plague you. Steer clear of this road. We've probably all been down it before yet found on it no permanent peace, and it can be endless. You may not be able to help yourself. Thinking, analyzing, figuring things out—these we do almost automatically. Take a turn down that road if you can't help yourself, but it would be best to avoid it. Try simply to observe what you see and hear, practice acceptance, and realize that you can't change the past or predict the future. Then sit and breathe. Let go of all that bogs you down, including analysis. And be honest. If the truth of what you find is painful to approach, be gentle with yourself, but don't run from the truth. It will continue to visit you even if you continue to deny it. But the sooner you look at it, the sooner you'll make peace with it. Embrace all of you, don't take life too personally, and your mind and heart will become open and free.

⑥ RESENTMENTS

Some of the mental anguish and confusion that we suffer comes from harboring resentments. This interferes with our spiritual progress. Resentments build up in us over time and can be much more destructive than simple anger. You will recognize resentment when you encounter it—if you are being honest with yourself. It carries with it a strong feeling of anger and indignation toward someone or something that you believe and feel has caused you harm. It is unrelieved, intense anger toward someone who has not given you what you want or has prevented you from being someone you want to be. It may start out as something small, but if not immediately attended to it can fester inside and grow out of proportion. Our parents, of course, are prime candidates for our resentment. The schools we went to, certain teachers, the IRS, our boss, the government, even God—all can be grist for our resentment mill.

While it is important to notice our resentments so that we can work on letting them go, be cautioned—resentments can be very seductive. If we're feeling badly about ourselves, we can sink into resentment and soothe our sore ego by blaming someone else for our predicament—it takes the focus off of us and places it outside of us, temporarily relieving us of emotional pain and convincing us that we are not responsible for whatever it is we are grappling with. We might resent our children for keeping us at home and away from a career or for draining our bank account. Maybe we resent our parents for not having the money to send us to the "right" school; or we resent our job for taking advantage of us, not challenging us as promised, and not paying us what we think we deserve.

Resentments come in many different forms. They can seduce us, blind us, convince us, motivate us, and delude us. Some of these consequences may not seem so bad at first. What's wrong, you might ask, with seduction or motivation? And that's exactly how resentments are designed to make you think. They blur reality, and the longer they sit with us the harder it is to touch the truth. All the noise and internal disturbance that resentments stir up cause such a commotion that we can hardly hear our usual, everyday chatter, let alone our deep voice of truth. When we sit with resentments brewing inside, it's like a radio stuck between stations, emitting only annoying and screeching static. So it is imperative to look at your resentments. You will learn to deal with them one by one. Eventually, they will be gone and your path will be cleared. If you allow them to hang around, they will only serve to interfere with your spiritual progress. If you don't address them, they will become a barrier to getting in touch with what you really want.

Doing internal housecleaning may seem daunting at first. But, as with everything else here, take it one task at a time, one moment at a time. No need to challenge yourself to more than you can handle in any given day. But don't allow that attitude to keep you from looking. Remember, take baby steps, tread lightly, breathe, and you'll find the courage.

So, let's take a look. Begin by asking yourself a simple question: Are you sitting with a minor irritation toward someone? Your boss, your wife, your child, or even the government? Write this person's name in your notebook. Now write out why you're peeved. What did they do? How did they hurt your feelings? What did they touch off in you? Have you ever had this feeling before? On what occasions? Write about those. Look at yourself honestly. Is the feeling that you're holding onto appropriate to the current situation? If so, that's fine. You're entitled to your feelings. If not, can you let go of the current resentment and place it back where it belongs? Maybe this feeling of resentment has nothing to do with current relationships and circumstances except on the surface. Chances are, especially if the resentment is intensely strong, it is probably attached to something or someone in your past that you haven't dealt with yet. We carry a lot of emotional baggage from our past, and much of this floats to the surface of our mind on the wave of a resentment and pollutes the present. So, as you become aware of your resentment, look closely for the source, and if it resides in the past then allow yourself to feel whatever this awareness encourages, and then let it go. Feel it, name it, observe its effect on you, then let it go. If it belongs in the here and now, can you practice letting it go anyway? Just for today, get it out of your heart and brain and turn to something else. Look at your role in the whole thing. What could you have done differently to avoid the anger or confrontation? What would make you feel better? What can you do for yourself to accomplish that? Write about all this.

This process of internal housecleaning—taking inventory, clearing out resentments—is just that, a process. It can't be done in a day or even a week. There is no way of knowing how long it will take. And that doesn't matter. As long as we understand how important it is to do it and make a commitment to continue the process, we've come a long way. So in the inventory section of your *Quiet Corner* notebook, write a letter to yourself about your commitment to the process of looking inside and being willing to face whatever you find. Write that letter now. Then begin to approach each of your resentments as it comes up and in your own time. Just as long as you do it. Start with the easy ones. As they disappear and allow the clouds in your mind to part, you will be able to see the more deeply rooted ones, the ones that influence and flavor each new one that arises. They can hurt you only if you continue to ignore them. Once revealed and written and spoken about, they will lose their power over you. The weight in your brain and heart will lighten. And the light of your spirit will brighten, and you will uncover the voice within that is eager to talk to you. Let it happen, and small and great wonders will be the reward for your efforts.

YOUR UNIQUENESS

To develop your self-awareness and get closer to your unique expression, in the inventory section of your *Quiet Corner* notebook set up a number of different sections. Here are some suggestions to include along with your resentment list:

1. FEELINGS At the top of a page write down a feeling that you are familiar with, such as sadness, anger, or joy. Each time you feel one, write on that page the specifics of why, when, who, and so on. Just write. When the page is full or when you have a half-dozen incidents, review the feeling. Is there a trend? Where are you in the equation? Make sure you write about your emotions and your resentments toward others. Get it out of your head and onto the page. Place the blame elsewhere if you want. Since you have no control over the behavior of others, ask yourself what you can do. There's no need to do anything yet, just write about it. Just introduce these ideas into your consciousness. Build up your awareness. Then start a solution page for each feeling. Write about how you think you could reverse the trend you see happening with a "negative" feeling and how you can promote more "positive" feelings.

2. FEARS This could turn out to be the most revealing part of the inventory-taking process, if you are honest with yourself. Being honest might not be easy for some of us and might take some doing. But keep at it. It's worth it in the end, for honesty will be

the wellspring for everything on this path, especially at this juncture.

First write down all the things, people, and situations you can think of that you hold some fear about. This first list may not be exhaustive; you can always come back to this exercise, but attempt to be thorough on this first go-round. Write down every little and big fear that you can think of. Your fear of cats, of being loved, of making mistakes, of snakes, of heights, of trusting, of failure. Anything that comes to mind. Then write about why you think you have this fear. Then write about how each fear infiltrates your life and how they collectively affect your sense of yourself and the way you interact in the world. How do these fears hold you back? Then look at what you bring to each situation, and think of what you might be able to do to alter the fear somewhat. Here is an example:

Fear: Talking in front of a large group
Why: Will be ridiculed as I was in grammar school, when others laughed at me when I read aloud.
Result today: Am timid in groups, hold myself back at work, lack ambition, avoid social situations where I don't know anyone
What I can do: My pride and anger are operating here and holding me back. I could make more of an effort to reach out and allow myself to feel uncomfortable; let people know that I'm uncomfortable rather than standing back, judging them, and feeling superior.

3. MONEY We can learn a lot about ourselves by looking at our relationship with money. Our attitude toward and behavior around money can inform us about our other relationships. If we are niggardly with our money, chances are we will be this

same way with our love, talents, affection, and heart. If we are spendthrifts, we might tend to give too much of ourselves away so that our gestures become meaningless, leaving us an empty shell. Write about your relationship with money and how you think it bleeds into other areas of your life. Consider your position on the following:

- Money would solve most/all of my problems.
- Once I settle my debt I'll be free to _____.
- I can't seem to save a dime.
- I can't afford to have fun.
- If I had all the money that I wanted I would_____.
- I worry about not having enough money.
- Most of my arguments with my partner involve money.

How do these things affect you in your everyday life? Write about this and be honest with yourself.

What insights did you have after doing this exercise? What can you do to change your money relationship? Here are some suggestions:

- For one week, put on the shelf all money arguments.
- Put $2.00 aside each day and buy some flowers at week's end. Do this for a month.
- Take one small action toward accomplishing something that you think lack of money keeps you from.
- Use your purpose tool each time a money worry crosses your mind, and say to yourself: "For right now, for today, at this moment, I have enough."
- Write a gratitude list of what you have each time the "I'll-never-get-what-I-want" thought pops up.

4. THE GOOD THINGS While it may seem that we have been focusing on our negative qualities, it is only because these are the ones that block us, that get in our way of living a serene, contented life in partnership with our God. But we must also look at our positive attributes, things about ourselves that boost our self-esteem, so we can create balance and keep from thinking that we are completely flawed. So make a list of the things you like about yourself. Ask your friends and family for their input, and begin to own this side of your personality. Here are some things you might say about yourself:

- ⑥ Considerate of others' feelings
- ⑥ Nearly always on time
- ⑥ Have a sense of humor
- ⑥ Have a talent for _____
- ⑥ Am generally willing to face new challenges

Fill at least one page in your *Quiet Corner* notebook, and return to it each time you feel your self-esteem flagging. Continue to add to it as you get to know yourself better.

Resentments, feelings, fears, money, the good things—five suggestions for self-inventory topics. Can you think of others? Write them down now. Keep track. This is not an easy process, but it is necessary if we want a clear head, an open heart, and an expressive inner voice.

PRAY UNTIL YOU MEAN IT

One simple tool to use in getting rid of resentments is prayer, especially directed toward the "guilty" party. When we are upset or angry, it is often difficult to feel charitable, but the more we practice, the easier it gets, and the benefits are glorious. So begin this practice with something simple. Let's start with a stranger. Is there someone famous whose achievement, money, fame, talent, or looks you envy? Be honest. Even if it's a small resentment or jealousy, use it. Now pray that this person receives even more of what it is you covet. Believe in your heart that they deserve that. Wish for them all the goodness that the universe can provide. Pray these prayers even if you don't mean it at first. Keep praying for this person. One day you will mean it. Your heart will open and your envy will disappear. Know that there is unlimited wealth in the universe and that the more others have, the more you will have.

Each time you acknowledge a resentment toward someone, pray for that person. Pray until you mean it. Pray, and your heart will become enriched and more loving. This love will nourish you on your journey and allow your heart to open even more, so that you can hear and trust your inner voice.

Do you ever get stuck in a mood where you're convinced that anyone else's life is more interesting than your own? Once you move through this feeling and get to the other side, do you sometimes wonder how you could have felt that way? When we are in a state of self-pity, self-centered fear, or self-loathing, nothing can dissuade us, even when we look at the facts of our lives— that we are not in touch with the truth. When we are sitting in such negative states we bury our inner voice beneath it all, and we lose our awareness of everything but this single obsession, whatever it may be at the time. So at such times it is a good idea to write your facts down. You need to be reminded of them. Do not focus on what you don't have. Enumerate the true facts of your life and try to disengage from the attached feelings. This will begin to move you out of your pool of negativity and into a state of gratitude.

Sometimes, however, the only solution is to move your body. Put on your exercise clothes and sneakers, drag yourself out the door, and start moving, one step at a time. By the end of your run or walk or bike ride, you'll feel much better. By next morning you'll be a different person, in a different, upbeat mood.

Moving your body is a crucial part of this process. It is one of the four key elements in the whole process, along with sitting and breathing, talking to others, and writing things down. There isn't a lot more to say about it except that it doesn't matter how you move, just move. You don't even have to move fast, just move. Walking, doing aerobics, running, swimming, practicing yoga, skating, dancing. Any movement will do. It can be fun; it's better if it is. This is not about getting in shape, though that can be a pleasant side effect. It is about just moving. Move your body, change your mind. Move your body, stir things up. If you are moving and concentrating on that, if you raise your heart rate and sweat some, your breath will move deeper. Whatever was on your mind will disappear or shift in some way. So if you're stuck in an obsessive mind struggle and nothing seems to be working, move your body. If you sink into negative thinking or the voices that don't belong to you get too loud, move your body. If you don't know what to do next, move your body. It will work.

SET A ROUTINE

Rather than waiting to be stuck in a groove of your mind before you move your body, why not establish a routine, a structure for movement. When my mind gets stuck and I realize I need to move my body to become unstuck, invariably it occurs when I've been neglecting regular exercise. So schedule some body movement time into your week. Don't set up an impossible schedule, and don't overdo it. If you haven't been exercising regularly, start small, one or two hours a week, fifteen or twenty minutes every two days. Build up to a comfortable level. If you have been working out, you might want to review how much time you spend on it. Sometimes we can go overboard and become obsessive/compulsive with it, especially if it feels good. That is not our goal here. Moving your body shouldn't take you away from yourself. It is meant to bring you closer. And, as with everything else, you need to establish some balance. So learn to balance your exercise and the lesson will spill over to the rest of your life.

6 · LEARN TO LISTEN, LISTEN TO LEARN

Most of us are poor listeners. However, before we can learn to listen to our own inner voice we need to learn to listen to others. Even though we have others' voices in our heads, it may not mean that we've really heard them or heeded them. It could just be background noise, filler, to keep us away from ourselves. And if you want to become a good listener, to tune into your own voice, it helps to practice by listening to others.

Do you tend to tune out what someone is saying to you as soon as you detect a tone of criticism? How about judgment? Or even praise? Or do you take these words to heart and believe even the worst that is said to and about you? You may not even know what you do, but every conversation you have with someone is an opportunity to learn something about yourself. So begin to pay attention. Take notice of how you converse with others. Do you always need to have the last word? Do you tend to offer a differing opinion just to have some fun? Do you dominate most conversations, or allow others to lead? How comfortable are you with silences? Do you find yourself resisting and rebutting constructive criticism or compliments? How thin or thick is your skin? Do other people's comments penetrate deeply or do they skim off your surface?

Start paying close attention to what people are saying to you. Become aware of your contribution or lack thereof. If you notice yourself reacting strongly to something that is said, pause and hold yourself back. Practice saying nothing. If you feel yourself withdrawing from a conversation or becoming bored, prick up your ears and join back in. At the end of each day, try to recall these instances and write about them. As you review each instance, try to remember exactly what the other person said. Do not judge it. Do not rewrite it. Then write about why you wanted to react or withdraw. Remember what was said, but then keep the focus on you. This is all meant to hone your awareness and bring you closer to hearing yourself. So listen to others and learn about yourself.

HOW WELL DO YOU LISTEN?

For one week, try this exercise: At the end of each day, choose one or two conversations that you had and try to re-create them on paper. Pay particular attention to what the other parties said. Be as accurate as possible. Keep your emotions at bay until you get down the words. How easy is this? Can you readily remember the content of the conversation?

Now write about how you felt while having the conversation. Reread the words of that conversation and write about how you now feel, eight or ten hours later. Is there a difference? What is it? Write about that. Did you react to the words said or the person saying them? Why? Did you listen well enough to hear what the person was saying? If not, can you hear it now? If you are having difficulty remembering the words but recall the feelings that a particular conversation stirred up in you, then write about that. Do these feelings have anything to do with what was said, or did you bring these feelings to the conversation? Would you have had them with or without the exchange? Where are they from? Write about them.

This exercise is simply a way of discovering how well we listen and what it is that interferes with that skill. It takes practice. So open your ears and let the world in.

WHAT'S IN A NAME?

How good are you at remembering names of people when you first meet them? If you have trouble here (and many people do), rather than seeing it as a deficiency, look at it as an opportunity to practice your listening skills. When you are introduced to someone, pay special attention to their name. Say it back to them when you say hello. If you forget it immediately, ask again what it is. Don't be embarrassed. There's a good chance they've also forgotten yours, and if you ask, they won't be shy about asking you. While you're at it, notice the color of their eyes, their hairstyle, or some other distinguishing characteristic. Make a mental note of it. At the end of the day, write down the names along with the special quality you noticed. Write a short paragraph about them, using their name often. If you haven't met any new people today, think back on some occasions when you did. Do you know the names of your local merchants? If you don't know their names but can visually recall these people, write a description of them or draw a picture. Ask their name the next time you see them. All of this is helpful in honing the skill of awareness. Also, knowing that you will be writing at the end of the day will encourage you to pay special attention. Before you know it, this skill will become second nature and you can bring it with you to your *Quiet Corner* as you get to know yourself on a deeper and more intimate level.

If remembering names is not difficult for you, try the exercise on something else. Describe your last vacation with specific details—names of streets or churches, colors in your room, the food you ate. Or how about the last book you read or movie you saw? Write some details about those. This can be fun and rewarding, so go for it! It will help you to begin paying attention to things, which will allow you to do what you're doing as you're doing it and not be off someplace in your mind thinking about something else. It will put you in the moment and heighten your enjoyment of everything.

The issue of control is very tricky. In this age of technology we have control over so much—changing TV channels without moving from our seat, retrieving phone messages even when away from home, sending e-mail messages across the globe. We tend toward delusion, thinking that we have control over most everything that happens or doesn't happen. We might even believe that we have some control over other people's behavior. If this is true it would follow that we certainly would have control over our own actions and behaviors. And to some extent this is all true. Anytime we interact with another human being we have some effect on them. We can make choices about how we behave. And until our machines break down we do have a certain amount of control over their operation.

But consider for a moment another possibility. Have you ever tried, by sheer willpower alone, to stay away from something or someone and been unable, no matter how sincere your desire, to keep to your vow? Have you ever decided, for example, to have just one more cookie and found yourself, three cookies later, feeling guilty, wondering what happened? Or do you, before you pick up the second cookie, throw all caution to the wind and say the heck with it, you'll start tomorrow, still believing in your heart that you made the decision, that you are in control? Have you ever been miraculously relieved of the compulsion to pick up that first cookie? Has the compulsion returned? Are you in charge of all this?

Wanting to be in control has everything to do with wanting what we want when we want it. It involves our ego and our belief that we know best. This to some degree is human nature, but when we allow this desire to control us, we become engaged in a struggle that we always lose. Since you've been practicing letting go, it is time now to look at what you want to control in your world and how you want to do that.

Are you unwilling to give up some of your responsibilities at work, even though you are overextended and work too long and too hard trying to get it all done? Do you think that no one can do as good a job as you, or that if you share the work it will be discovered that your approach hasn't been ideal? This inability to let go is a clue that you are trying to control things. Anytime you feel yourself holding on, resisting change, consider that a control issue is lurking in the background.

Do you always have an opinion about how other people throw dinner parties, raise their children, conduct their personal relationships? If you hold the notion that your way is the right way to do things, it's a clue that you want to control things. Anytime you are critical of others consider that a control issue is lurking in the background.

Do you have trouble trusting people? Do feelings of jealousy invade your mind when your spouse is away from home or even when he talks to another woman in your presence? Do you worry yourself sick whenever your children are away from you? If any of this resonates with you there may be a control issue lurking in the background. Anytime you cling to someone or something, your need to control is engaged, or vice versa.

Are you ever aggravated when your favorite TV program is preempted by a previously unannounced substitute? Do your mother-in-law's opinions continue to oppress and anger you? When the world doesn't cooperate with your plan or when people continue to push your buttons even when you admit you have no control over any of it, if you continue to react with scorn or frustration there is probably a control issue lurking in the background. Anytime your mood is negatively affected by someone else's behavior it probably means that they are not doing what you want, which means you are not in control but want to be.

Start keeping track of your control issues—your need to control people, circumstances, outcomes. Each time you identify one, pick up your purpose tool, look around you, notice some detail, bring your attention to your breath, and take three deep breaths. Then practice letting go. Let go of your need to control. For the moment. You will not be perfect at this exercise, but you will learn a great deal about yourself by looking at your need to control. If you think this doesn't apply to you in any way, then move on. But anytime you are upset, short tempered, aggravated, or depressed, consider that control might be the issue, and then come back to yourself. Write about it, breathe, let go, and turn it over. If this doesn't work, just breathe. You're doing that anyway, so just pay attention to it. Let your breath take charge of you for a few moments. Give yourself a break. By the time you return to normal mode, your need to control will have lessened. And you will be more available to yourself, free to continue on your *Quiet Corner* journey. If you stay stuck in control mode, none of this will work, and your inner voice will be lost to you. So become aware of your control issues. Then let them go. And move on.

DO SOMETHING OUT OF CHARACTER

In the inventory part of your notebook, start a section on control. For one week, each time you become aware of an upset or an obsession or some compulsive behavior, record the incidents in your notebook and look at them as they relate to control. Once you become aware of your need to control (and this may happen before you even begin writing), look at what this need is connected to. Is it fear, or greed, or depression? Write about why these feelings ignite your need to control. Little by little, when you're ready, begin practicing the art of letting go. Give up your need to go to the mountains for vacation; instead go to the seashore where your partner wants to go. Be charitable and generous. Try to make it not matter, but don't become a martyr. Stop telling your son or daughter or husband how to drive when you're in the passenger seat. Do these things with good intentions and love. If you can't quite get to those feelings when you begin, then practice as if you felt them. For one week, let other people in your life make the decisions, if they want to. Turn it over to them. Just go along. On the other hand, if your version of control is letting others do it all for you, then begin to take charge of things. Surprise your loved ones. Do something out of character. You might even begin to enjoy it. You might even surprise yourself.

As you take inventory and get in touch with what goes on inside, much of what you've uncovered and stirred up will continue to rise up each time you retreat to your *Quiet Corner* to sit and breathe. Don't be alarmed, and don't try to control it. Just let it come. This is part of the process. You might have reached a stage in sitting where you're able to attain a peaceful state and sit undisturbed for a stretch of time.

As you look deeper inside and your serenity becomes disturbed, you might feel that rather than moving forward, you're slipping backward. Although it may feel that way, that is not the truth. There will often be times when you can't seem to sit still, when your thoughts and feelings begin to overwhelm you. Use these times as opportunities to strengthen your practice and learn even more about yourself. Each time is an opportunity to go deeper into yourself. The mental disturbance is just a sign of greater self-awareness. Use it. Don't judge yourself. Just breathe. Allow the thoughts and feelings to rise up, and then practice letting go. Even when they come fast and furious, sit still and concentrate even harder on your breathing. Count your breaths. Engage in the battle with your thoughts and sit them out. Let them come at you one at a time, until there's nothing left.

If you have a particularly difficult and brain-noisy session of sitting, write about it in your notebook. What came up for you that you just couldn't let go of? Why are you so attached to these thoughts? Write about that. You might want to sit again after you've written about it to see if anything has changed. Or take particular notice the next time you sit. Write about the changes. Continue this process of self-awareness. The first stage is the most intense and painful. But even this process never ends. We are so complex that no matter how long we live, there will always be something to learn. So keep sitting, keep breathing, and keep looking inside to get to a deeper self-awareness and to your pure and true inner voice.

BOOK II

Acceptance

5

Sharing Yourself

⑥ TALKING OUT LOUD

Sitting silently, listening to yourself and others, practicing these two things daily, honing your attentiveness, your concentration, your breathing—these are all critical to *Quiet Corner* practice and to finding your voice. But it is also important, as you progress along this path, to recognize and accept your limitations and the obstacles that you have contrived to put in your own way, and to let them go. One way to do this is to name things and speak them out loud.

When we keep ideas, fears, anger, even joy trapped inside our brain, inside our bodies, they become bigger than they are. They become negative energy. Writing is one important tool to help sort out these various obstacles and find the right words for them. But don't let it stop there. These things need to be expressed, spoken, out loud.

Hearing yourself say the words will transform the power that they hold over you. They will no longer have the energy to hold you hostage. They will fizzle out and quickly lose energy. You will be surprised how fast and powerful this is, releasing words out into the universe. The results are immediate. And you can begin by yourself, in the privacy of your own home. You might feel silly at first, talking out loud to yourself, but after you begin (and you know that is the hard part) you will become accustomed to the sound of your own voice. Who knows, you may even learn to like it.

There are many different ways to begin this exercise, but, as always, start small. Just so you don't feel too self-conscious, you might want to begin by talking into a tape recorder. This will make it less daunting and will give you the added bonus of being able to play back what you've said. Our recorded voices always sound different from the way we hear ourselves, so you may learn something valuable about yourself by doing this. And it can be fun.

Yell, chant, sing, use different accents. These are ways to entice yourself into talking out loud. You might want to start by reading other people's words aloud. Choose a favorite poem and read to your sweetheart, just to get used to your nonconversational voice. Each morning, after writing down your dreams, read them out loud to your partner or to yourself. Anytime you find yourself obsessing about anything, write it down and then say it aloud. The obsession will ease. Anytime you confront one of your fears, write it down and then say it aloud. Do this with anything that nags you. Send it into the universe through your vocal cords. Though you may not be able to handle it, the universe will. It may return, but it will return softer and gentler. Let it go again and again if necessary. Pretty soon, you'll discover that it's gone for good.

BANG A DRUM

Take the list of fears that you wrote in your personal inventory and create a rhyming poem out of them. It doesn't have to make sense (in fact, the more nonsensical the better), and no one else need read it. Then recite it out loud. Put it to music. Make a rap song out of it. Sing it. Or make a chant, beat a drum (or the bottom of a wooden bowl), and let loose. Take these troublesome, fearsome words from deep inside you and release them into the big, wide universe. It will take them from you, and they will merge into the collective energy pool. They will lose their power over you. They may not disappear completely the first time you do this, but eventually they will be gone. You will see how the emphasis shifts and the intensity shrinks each time. Do this exercise with anything that feels overwhelming, one word at a time. If you turn it into a fun exercise each time, it may be easier to approach. Use the writing exercises that you've done so far as a starting point. Talk out loud about your dreams. Talk out loud about your fears. Talk out loud to your pet if that helps. It doesn't matter where or how, just open your throat and start moving your lips.

Growing up in a large family, with seven siblings and very little money, I was taught very early about sharing. Rarely was there more than enough to go around, so we each had to take only our share; if we were given something that the others weren't, we were expected to share it. My older sister's clothes were shared with me after she outgrew them.

But I don't remember being encouraged to share my feelings or my inner self. If we children needed to talk about something that my parents had no experience with, we were in many different ways steered away from whatever it was that was bothering us. Eventually we stopped trying and kept our "private" feelings to ourselves.

Today, people share intimate details of their lives on national TV. Unfortunately, this is done mostly for shock value and ratings (and money!). Rarely is the individual handled with care. I think that many of us have difficulty sharing ourselves with another human being, yet it is crucial to our spiritual development to learn to share ourselves with others. (We must proceed with caution, however, as we don't need to expose ourselves unnecessarily to an inappropriate person.)

First, it is important to speak about our inner workings out loud. You may think that you already do this, and many of us do to some extent when we confide in our best friends and lovers. But this kind of sharing doesn't always get to our core. We might relate our sadness and frustration about a troubling relationship, for instance, but we might not get in touch with our contribution to the problem. And while our supportive friends may offer their shoulder to cry on, they do not point out our flaws, nor should they. During the inventory-taking process you will discover your so-called flaws and other things about yourself that you might like to keep secret. Sharing these deep, dark secrets with someone else is what is important here.

Second, we cannot always make sense of our life, so we need to include another compassionate human being in our process. (The selection of this person is critical and discussed in more detail in the following chapters.) As we learned earlier, we cannot make progress on this path without the help of a higher power, nor can we move forward without feeling part of the human race. Confiding in another person is the most potent way of doing this.

Third, by including a third party (after you and your God), you can practice sharing and allowing yourself to "make mistakes." By doing this you will learn how to open your heart to others and share yourself with the universe.

Fourth, this practice of sharing yourself with one other person will teach you many things, and you will hear your voice in a way that you cannot hear it otherwise.

If you are feeling detached from your life, angrier than usual without knowing exactly why, quieter, or more vocal than usual, chances are some voices inside you have to be heard and released from their internal prison. Sometimes, no matter how hard you work at it, you may not be able to hear them on your own. This is why it is so important to talk out loud to someone else, especially if you don't even know what you want to say.

We often don't know what our inner voice is saying until we open our mouth and hear the words. Most of the time we're surprised at what comes out, even though we know it to be the truth. The risk of not doing this is great. Being scared and uncomfortable about it is normal. If we don't speak out loud and set free our inner thoughts and fears, we run the risk of allowing these inner beings to grow bigger and more burdensome than is healthy. They can transform themselves into demons that squelch and overpower our deep and pure inner voice, the wellspring for our soul.

So do yourself and your true voice a favor. Speak out, talk to someone else, let go of the false and ego-driven voices that cloud your purity. These false voices are sent to you as challenges; you need to conquer them to free your real voice. Beware of thinking that these voices are your truth. They can be very seductive. Left alone, they grow out of proportion. You need to bounce your ideas, thoughts, and fears off someone else from time to time. Other people can give you some perspective and act as a reality check.

Since this practice of sharing yourself may be new, it will take time to clear out the layers that have accumulated over the years. But be diligent and patient. This is an important step, and the rewards are great. As you gain experience, you will clear away the hard layers that have both protected and interfered with your inner voice. Also, as new voices enter your consciousness and new fears and feelings come to light, you will become aware of them before they have time to become entrenched.

This process of identifying and letting go of what does not belong to the truth of your essence is ongoing and takes practice. But before you know it, letting go will become as natural as storing these voices once was. So allow yourself to feel awkward, embarrassed, and uncomfortable as you talk out loud and say the words that need saying. One day, you will speak your real truth. As you and your listener get used to hearing your voice, the truth will reveal itself. Look forward to that day, trust that it will come, and just keep talking.

⑥ TALKING TO AND LEARNING FROM OTHERS—SPIRITUAL FRIENDS AND MENTORS

Though often in the company of others, many of us not only believe that we can get by on our own, we rarely ask for help from someone else. We learn to keep our personal issues to ourselves. Whatever happens inside the privacy of our heart, brain, and home is our business. We think that it just isn't right to talk about it in the outside world.

But, as the saying goes, no man is an island—we belong to the human community, and we all need each other. We need to seek out mentors who will guide us along the path of our spirit. At a certain point, we cannot go it alone.

By reaching out and trusting another human being, everything changes. We become vulnerable, our heart opens wide. We lighten our burden, and the edges of our world become softer. We achieve a feeling of belonging, we give and receive love without thought, and our center settles into itself. All this, just by opening ourselves to another human being and sharing our deepest selves.

If you have a group of friends who are interested in traveling this road with you, you might want to start a weekly or monthly *Quiet Corner* sharing group. I would suggest making it a same-gender group, as many of the issues that come up will be of such a nature that you might not feel as open in a mixed group—this is part of choosing well (unfortunately, everyone you know cannot be trusted with your secrets). When you meet, give each person a chance to talk out loud about their present state of mind. Take one of the writing exercises in this book and write together. Then share with each other, out loud, what you've written. Assign a writing exercise between meetings and share what you've written at the next. Start at the beginning of the suggested exercises and work your way through to the end together. Write about your fears one week, your relationship with your mother, father, or spouse the next, and then write a poem or a short story that describes your relationship with money. Use your collective imagination and create exercises that go beyond the ones suggested here. As you grow with each other, your trust will build, and you will learn to unconditionally support each other. Leave your judge, critic, and need to gossip at the door. Make a pact with the group that everything said will be confidential among the members. This will give each of you the courage to reveal all of yourself. Remember that you are only as sick as your secrets. So let them out and enjoy good spiritual and emotional health.

You may find as you get deeper into this process that you'd rather not share certain things with a group. That's fine and understandable. But don't keep them to yourself. Find one person you trust to share them with, such as a minister or good friend. Just as long as you let it out and put it in someone else's ear, it matters not who that person is so long as there is trust. Take your time in choosing, and start slowly. You will soon know whether you've chosen well. Keep trying if the first choice fails. You are learning as you go—about yourself, others, trust, sharing. Don't think of bad choices as bad, think of them as lessons, and move on.

At some point along your journey you might want to add a spiritual mentor to your box of *Quiet Corner* tools. This would be someone who you could consult regularly as you move along your spiritual path, someone who could help monitor your spiritual growth. Sometimes, we need a mirror to see ourselves. A spiritual mentor can be a mirror for you to see your spiritual progress. This person might have a spiritual demeanor that you admire, or maybe has walked the path ahead of you and can help guide you along the way. Spiritual mentors can help you avoid making some of the mistakes they made and help you navigate your way through the rough spots.

Your mentor could be a friend whom you trust entirely, or a religious advisor or professional therapist. But be careful as you begin to confide in and rely on this person that you don't set them up as a god or a guru. This will only lead to disappointment, for they are only human. Use this person as a tool, a guide, a spiritual friend, a confidant. But remember that in the end you must rely on you and your inner voice. That will be the ultimate truth for you.

It might be beneficial to choose more than one person to confide in. Even if you find someone you trust to speak with regularly, especially if this person also shares deeply with you about him- or herself, things will come up that you will need to talk to someone else about. This will also help you avoid relying too heavily on any one person and running the risk of deifying them.

Don't become insulated and rigid in this process. Keep your heart and mind open. This is the key here. If you are open, your spiritual mentors will reach you and you will recognize them when they appear. It is said that when the student is ready, the teacher will appear. So don't skip this step. Even if it takes time to get here. Keep talking and sharing and writing. Think of it as a circular rather than linear process. Throw yourself in and sail round to self-awareness and serenity.

YOUR QUIET CORNER GROUP

If you decide to start a *Quiet Corner* sharing group, here are some suggestions.

- Establish a time structure. Determine how long you want each session to last and stick to it. Begin and end on time.

- Keep the group open to new members. Once you're well on your way along this path, you can learn a great deal from the neophyte as well as be there as a guide.
- No one should become the boss. You are all equal and learning from each other.
- Establish a format for the group. Perhaps members can take turns starting the group with a favorite prayer. Save some time at the end of each session for socializing and perhaps some tea, but keep to the purpose of the meeting during the time allotted or you'll see it slip away before you know it.
- Encourage a ritual to develop. Light incense and candles.
- Allow each person equal time to share, but remain open to the possibility that one person might need more than her share of time on a given night. Give it to her. Next week you might have the same need.
- Be flexible. Be loving. And keep sharing.

PROFESSIONAL HELP—
IS IT FOR EVERYONE?

There may come a time in your spiritual development when you'd like to consult with a professional. Sharing with peers or even someone further along the road is important, and professional help does not replace this. But sometimes we hit a particularly rocky part of the road that calls for an expert to help smooth out. This is not necessary for everyone, nor is it a "bad" sign if it does become necessary. We each have our own particular surface to travel and different experiences that affect our movement. Some issues are more deeply entrenched than others, and some we can gain no perspective on without help. Don't by shy. Don't judge yourself. Do what you must to get through.

If you decide to seek out a professional therapist, be careful whom you choose. Ask around. Interview them. If you feel any hesitation or if there is a question in your mind, move on to the next. But remember that you will have a certain amount of trepidation no matter what. It's not easy to open yourself to a stranger, even if she is a professional. Be aware of what is real and how much your fear is playing a role. Begin to trust your instinct and listen to what your gut is saying. You've come far enough to know this much. Trust yourself and then put your trust in the professional.

Once you've established a relationship, don't let your other sharing relationships slip away. Keep nurturing those. Use the therapeutic relationship to share what you can't share elsewhere. Work it out, and then move on. When you get to another block, go back. Keep this up until there are no blocks left or until you've learned to move them out of your way yourself. Share it with a friend, share it with a therapist, share it with a spiritual teacher, share it with a religious leader. Share yourself and hear yourself sharing.

Looking at your resentments and fears, sharing them with someone else, exposing yourself to another, feeling vulnerable and flawed—confronting the truth of yourself takes a lot of courage, and many days you will simply not be up to it. Sometimes you'll need to take a break from yourself and this process of self-examination. Escape to the movies. Spend the weekend at a spa being pampered. Turn your brain off, if you can. Allow yourself a reprieve and wait until your heart feels strong and willing before returning.

But be careful. Some things that take us away from ourselves and the reality of our lives can be dangerous and can keep us away longer than is healthy. Many people turn to drugs, alcohol, work, or sex to escape from themselves but can get caught in the cycle of addiction and never return. So take a break if you must, but quickly return to the process, even if you are accompanied by fear and anxiety.

Check your motives before running. Anytime you hear yourself saying "If only . . . ," look a little closer. Do you want to leave your job and look for another because the current one holds no more challenges for you, or because you can't get along with your boss (she doesn't value you or your opinions enough)? Do you hear yourself saying: "If only she would just let me . . ."? Do you want to leave your partner because you have truly grown apart, or because he no longer fits your image of him? Do you hear yourself saying: "If only he would just . . ."? Do you want to stop looking inside because it hurts too much, or because you think none of it is your fault anyway, so why bother? Do you hear yourself saying: "If only my life . . ."?

When you want to run away because the people in your world are not behaving the way you'd like them to, it is time to practice acceptance of them. You cannot change what they do or how they choose to do it, you can only accept them. Remember, you have no control over the workings of the world, so acceptance is the only recourse. Accept, then look back to yourself, the only one whose behavior you can affect. Look back, and then share what you find.

This stage of looking inside and sharing what you find is one of the most difficult ones, but once you're through it, you're through it. You don't have to pass this way again with such intensity. So pluck up your courage, and each time you become aware of your desire to run away, sit with yourself for a few minutes. Don't simply react to the impulse. Practice some acceptance. By now, your self-awareness will be heightened—you will know whether this need to run is simply a healthy need to take a break. If it stems from fear, it's still okay to check out for a while, but be aware that it might be harder to return. Don't wait for all the fear to dissipate before coming back. Be honest and rigorous in every aspect of this process, and you will be rewarded beyond measure.

So, be a kid again, pack your bags and run away from home, if only in your imagination. Have a ball, loosen up, kick back, and return home to yourself, refreshed and ready to continue—a little wiser, a little freer, a little more willing. And a lot more accepting.

⑥ BRINGING YOURSELF INTO THE PRESENT

When uncovering and facing your demons, your shortcomings, the old layers of your false being, there is danger of living too much in the past. Sometimes we get trapped in its web and convince ourselves that we can change or recover our past. But we can't, and if we're honest with ourselves we probably don't really want to anyway. What we really want is to make peace with it— simply accept it and put it behind us. And that is what this process promises you.

But, being human, we are sometimes more comfortable in the past (because it is known and not scary) or the future (because that can be anything our creative mind wants it to be). But neither the past nor the future is where we need to be if we truly want to hear our inner voice. By spending time in our minds in either the past or the future, we can't hear our inner voice because we're too busy conjuring up something that does not exist now. Our only chance of hearing our voice occurs when we sit firmly in the now.

The past is over; the future isn't here yet. Even though we all know this, we still must force ourselves to be in the present moment. This is the only real time there is. This is where everything happens. This is where you live, whether you're aware of it or not. So better be in it and aware, than in it and not.

Always practice bringing yourself into the present moment. Use your purpose tool. Where are your feet? What are your hands doing? What color are your socks? Each time you share yourself with your chosen spiritual guide, begin and end with a few moments of concentrated breathing. Bring your awareness to your breath and to the present moment. Know that going back into your past is an important exercise, but once you speak your words, let that be it, don't dwell on them, don't carry them around, let them go. Even if they don't go away the first time you speak them, don't despair. Say them again next time. Each time it will be easier. Each time the impact will be smaller. Soon they will be gone. Don't think about when. Don't think about time. Breathe and be with yourself in this moment. Feel the ground under your feet. Breathe the fresh air around you. Notice the different smells in the room or park you are in. Hold your friend's hand. Be aware of the touch of that person, the feel of skin to skin. Say a prayer that reminds you of this moment. Find one and read it, or compose one of your own.

What is important about this moment? Write for a few minutes and describe the scene in front of you. Be aware that as soon as you put the words down on paper, the scene has changed, you have changed. It is like a flowing river. Choose a spot to look at. Notice how you cannot keep it in one place. It constantly moves and changes. So does your life. Each moment is new and fresh and different. Be there for each moment, and your life will be as clear and strong as a river. Practice this throughout the day. Think of yourself and all that surrounds you as the river. Go with the flow and breathe your way from one moment to the next, keeping the past behind you and the future in front. And enjoy the journey.

6

More
Letting Go

WHEN YOU POINT ONE FINGER, THREE ARE POINTING BACK AT YOU (OR, MIND YOUR OWN BUSINESS)

Point your finger. Make the gesture with your hand and point your finger at the wall. Now look at your hand as it is pointing. Chances are your index finger is pointing at the wall and your other three fingers are curled back into your palm. One finger is pointing away from you, three are pointing back at you. This is only a hand gesture, but it's a good image to keep in mind anytime you place blame, criticize, judge, mock, or otherwise send negative thoughts and energy out toward another person. Whenever you do this, be aware that whatever you are feeling or thinking comes from something inside you that has been stirred up. The other person is only the catalyst. You are responsible for your feelings, not them. No one else has power over you and your feelings unless you give it to them. So it is important, each time you notice yourself pointing a finger, to turn it around and look at yourself. Keep the focus on yourself. Mind your own business.

Turning your attention inward and looking at yourself does not mean that your feelings toward the pointed-at subject are not warranted, nor does it call for you to negate your feelings. It means that you should bring them home, where they belong. It means that you should own these feelings; they belong to you and no other. Anytime you are disturbed by something outside yourself, it means that something is going on inside you. It is an opportunity to look closer, to dig deeper, to get to know yourself better. Sometimes it's hard to look, especially when we're upset. We'd rather place the blame outside—on something or somebody we have no control over—than look at our part in it.

My friend Leslie has recently been learning graphic design on a computer. She is a very skilled artist and designer at the bottom of a new learning curve with computer design. She had been working on a small project for a friend to practice her skills. In the process, she lost a disk that had on it some valuable information not stored in the computer. Slightly frantic, she searched her desk and files and came up with nothing. Then she was convinced that someone else had it—the friend she was doing the project for, another friend who had helped with it, maybe the print shop she had used. She couldn't find it, gave it up for lost, and was sure it wasn't in her office. Someone else was at fault. Later that week, turning her attention to her taxes (she had been procrastinating for months), she found the missing disk buried under piles of paper on her desk. She had put it in a neatly labeled folder but then lost it in her income tax heap.

Leslie wasted a lot of energy through all this, but she also learned a great deal about herself. She learned that procrastination in one area of her life spills over into others and creates chaos. She learned that taking an action in one unmanageable part of her life benefits other areas. She saw how her financial insecurity and fear of the future create problems but that making a start on something that seems overwhelming causes the pressure to lessen and makes the task seem doable. And she learned that no matter what, no one else is responsible for her chaos. Today, Leslie is further along the computer learning curve, so her anxiety has subsided; she made great headway on her taxes, so her fear decreased; and she knows that as long as she keeps the focus on herself and what she must do, her life will be smoother and less chaotic.

As Leslie relieved herself of the burden of fear and anxiety around her work and taxes, she became more available to herself. She was no longer caught in the powerful grip of self-doubt. This freed her to relax and begin to accept and trust herself again. Her inner voice was no longer in a stranglehold and was available once more to express itself through her work and her art.

When we point our finger, we look outside ourselves for an explanation of whatever it is that's going on inside. And just as we can't be spiritually satisfied by looking outward, we can't understand ourselves and hear our voice if we direct our attention to others in a negative way. So, before pointing your finger (even if in your heart you know it's the other person's fault), ask yourself if you've done all you can, even ask the other person what you can do. Put it on your side of the fence (without playing the victim), and look at your need to point the finger. Get in touch with why you need to take the attention off yourself. What is going on inside you? Write about it, talk about it, pray about it. If you keep the focus on yourself and your contribution to the situation, clarity will follow. And isn't that all we're looking for? Keep your fingers to yourself and the rewards will be forthcoming.

WHOSE VOICE IS THAT INSIDE YOUR HEAD? WHOSE FEELING IS THAT INSIDE YOUR HEART?

An extreme form of mind noise is obsession, an anxious and often irrational preoccupation with someone or something. If you are prone to obsession, then you know what this feels like and how distracting it can be. If this state rarely visits you, well, lucky you. Even though we usually view obsession as negative, it has some positive qualities, and we can learn and gain from it.

Do you ever want something or want to be rid of something so badly that you can think of nothing else? Your thinking becomes distorted and singularly focused, you can't sleep at night for thinking about it? Your appetite is affected, you find no joy in the everyday, you might even become dysfunctional in your everyday life, everything reminding you of this thing that you do or do not have. Do you fall into a state of depression and self-pity? While this litany of symptoms is an extreme description of an obsessive condition, perhaps you've experienced a milder version of this. Either way, you probably continue to operate in the normal world no matter how mild or extreme your version is, and you probably convince yourself that "if only" you had or were rid of that something all would be well. And that might be true. But consider for a moment how you appear in the world in such an obsessive condition.

You may believe that no one notices because you keep the obsessive thoughts to yourself. You daydream at work wondering if he's called, when he'll call, what you'll say when he does. You keep calling your voice mail to check messages. You wish you still smoked so that you could relax with a cigarette. Craving becomes stronger, and you almost convince yourself that if you started smoking you'd lose the ten extra pounds that you're carrying, which is probably the reason he's not calling. If only you had married last year when you had the chance, or not gotten divorced, you wouldn't be feeling this way. Your life would be better because you'd be married and not sitting around waiting for his call, for Prince Charming to come and save you from a lonely existence.

In this state, and in any state along the obsession spectrum, we create walls that send a signal to the world that we are not fully at home, that we are lost in the quagmire of self-centeredness. When we are obsessed with anything—an idea, a person, a thing—we leave no room for that idea to expand, for that person to enter our life, for the possibility of having that thing. We become so attached to the *desire* that there's no space left for the real thing. If we're obsessed with the Prince Charming who isn't calling, we can't notice the one who just walked in the door. While this is a perfect opportunity for hopelessness to visit, it is also a perfect opportunity to go deeper and become freer. Whenever you arrive at this state, whatever its intensity, exert your will and open your eyes to your true nature. See how your will, desire, and ego got you to this place.

Desire, expectations, and a needy ego combine to create an obsession. We convince ourselves not only that we deserve this thing or person that has become the object of our obsession but that by getting it our lives would be transformed, our needs satisfied, and our hopes realized. But an obsession is something that is all but unobtainable, and by letting it control us and create havoc with our moods and general state of being we set ourselves up for disappointment and a bruised ego. When you live in obsession, you run away from the things you have. Perhaps you're afraid to enjoy what you have or feel you aren't worthy of all the gifts life has given you. Use this opportunity to explore that possibility and to truly understand yourself and your own motivations. Perhaps there's a voice telling you that it's wrong to experience happiness or satisfaction with things the way they are. Explore that. Whenever obsession strikes, ask to be relieved of the burden of self. Know that relief will come if you ask for it and that grace will appear and assist you in letting go.

This is not to say that you must stop caring. Obsession and caring are not synonymous. It is possible to care about something or someone after being relieved of the obsession. Once we stop obsessing, we become open to the miracle of life. We ease up and relax, allowing new thoughts and people to approach us. Our walls come down and our hearts fall open. Our inner voice becomes louder and clearer. We are ready to receive the gifts of the universe, the ones waiting for us, the ones we could not even imagine, let alone desire, for ourselves.

So don't seek out an obsession, and don't feel defeated if it arrives. Let it run its course. Practice using all your tools, pray to be relieved of the obsession, and be willing to move to the other side of it, the side with light, the side with possibility, the side where your true voice, your pure heart, resides. Obsess, but don't live in it. Feel the hurt, but don't feed it. Breathe. Accept all of you. And then *just listen*.

PEOPLE, PLACES, THINGS

Make a list of the elements you feel are missing from your life, the things you don't have but spend a considerable amount of time thinking and dreaming about. Make another list of all the elements you do have but feel you cannot let go of. Look back at your personal inventory and list of resentments to remind yourself of things you are holding on to. Here are some areas to look at and include in this process:

People
Places
Things
Fears
Desires
Feelings
Attitudes
Being Right
The Past
The Future
Money
Sex
Likes
Dislikes
Habits
Anger

After making these lists, ask yourself how important each element is to you. What would you gain by getting what you don't have? What would you lose by letting go of what you do have? Write about each attachment. What are your motives? Where are you in all of it?

THE GIFTS OF LOSS

Choose two things from the previous exercise—one that you don't have yet and one that you do. Now imagine never getting the first and losing the second. Write about the holes each would leave in your life, the spaces that would exist. Then write about what that space means to you. Follow these two losses to a conclusion. After writing about and experiencing the grief that each loss would bring, can you imagine the aftermath, the sun after the storm, the flip side of grief and the potential joy that each loss might bring? Write about it. Have you ever lost anything dear to you? Write about that experience. Were you ever able to receive the gifts of that loss, or did you cling to the pain of it? Write, write, and write some more.

Then sit quietly and absorb what you've uncovered here. This is all big stuff. This is all about going deeper, learning about yourself and what makes you you. You won't like everything you find, but maybe you'll love the uniqueness of it, the uniqueness of you. Remember, you can just simply let go of what you see that you no longer want. You've learned by now how to do that. Accept it as yours and then set it free.

As you sit and breathe and think about what you'd like to be rid of, give each one a shape inside you. Visualize this shape sprouting wings and flying away from you out through the crown of your head. Let it go. Sit and breathe. Experience what the loss feels like. Wish it well as it flies away on its journey into freedom as you sit there breathing, a little lighter, a little freer yourself. And then congratulate yourself. This is not easy. You will not get rid of all your attachments at once. It may take a few tries to rid yourself of even one. But congratulate yourself for trying. Congratulate yourself for being willing. As long as you keep it up, your attachments will go. Maybe not in your time, but certainly in your God's time.

WHEN ONE DOOR CLOSES, ANOTHER OPENS

We often get stuck in the feeling of grief and self-pity when we lose something dear to us. It is a common human reaction to loss. We've talked about the need to let go of the people and things we're attached to so we can better appreciate them while we have them. Yet when we lose something, even if we've practiced letting go before losing it, we might continue to cling to it in our mind and heart after it disappears. Letting go is critical at the point of loss, for if we hang on to the disappeared we leave no space for something new to enter and take its place. Even when we successfully let go and invite new things in when we lose big things, it may not be so easy to do with the smaller things in life.

I've lost loved ones, cherished jobs, important relationships over the years. And while each loss was devastating and traumatic in its own way, I came through to the other side of each, appreciating the loss and acknowledging the gifts that followed in its wake. With each new loss and subsequent gift, I've learned to let go sooner and look for the new door to open. Practice has helped me to shorten the time between one door closing and another opening.

I thought I was getting pretty good at it, too, until recently, when after sitting for my usual forty-five-minute period I had a minor epiphany as I was eating breakfast staring out the window. I am lucky to live in an apartment in New York City that is quiet and filled with light. Birds outside my windows can sometimes chirp so loudly I forget that I am in the middle of one of the largest, noisiest cities in the world. And I am grateful each day when I hear their song. Since moving into this apartment six years ago, one of the best features has been the huge trees outside my large living room windows; in addition to being beautiful scenery, these trees hid from view two ugly buildings across the way. Spring was always an especially beautiful season as the green deepened and expanded, invading my apartment with the color of nature and filling my view with beauty. I never took these trees for granted, and I felt grateful each time I walked through my apartment, especially when it was warm enough to have the windows open. This past spring, after coming home from an extended trip and looking forward to being back, I thought of the trees and wondered what state of bloom they would be in. As soon as I walked in, I felt that something was wrong. My apartment felt stripped of something precious. The trees were gone. Just gone!

I couldn't believe it. My heart broke. I was angry, sad, furious, disbelieving, hurt, appalled. Many feelings attacked me. I learned that the neighboring building manager cut them down because one tree was leaning over the fence that divides the properties and he was afraid of an accident followed by a possible lawsuit. He cut them all down! I went through the spring and summer months missing those trees. I never got over the hurt. I thought about moving. I didn't like being at home much anymore. When people visited I talked about the missing trees and always at some point remarked, "You should have seen it when. . . ." I couldn't let go and thought I had every right to hang on.

Recently, while I was sitting and eating my cereal, I noticed how blue the sky was and how white the few clouds. The plane in the distance caught my attention. I was surprised to see so much sky and realized that all this time I had been missing the trees I hadn't looked beyond the hole that was made to see the sky. For months, I missed the sky because I missed the trees. Very few New Yorkers can see a lot of sky from their windows. How lucky I felt. Here was the new door opening. Why hadn't I seen it sooner? Well, I see it now and am grateful again for my home and the nature that sits in full view outside my window. A small thing, but a big lesson.

CLOSED DOORS, OPEN WINDOWS

Are you hanging on to the idea of something that you lost in actuality but can't quite let go of in your mind? How about these:

- Youth
- One summer experience against which all others pale
- Your first love (this is a tricky one because our first love will always be special; but do you use it as a benchmark for all others?)
- A relationship
- A treasured book that you loaned to a friend
- Your ability to move around the squash court the way you once did
- A career in a field that you loved (you chose instead a more lucrative but less fulfilling career)
- A job offer
- A promotion at work

Can you think of others? Write them down. Think about some smaller ones. Do you have any that are equivalent to my trees? Write them down. Then write about each, about how you hang on and what you might be obscuring from your view by doing so. Work with these one at a time, and practice letting go. Don't wait for the new door to open before letting go. Let go and trust that there will be one. You may have to walk through a long, empty hall before getting to the next door, but there's lots to be gained in the waiting. Accept the loss. Accept the wait. Accept the new gift. You will breathe and sleep easier.

Nothing is either fully black or white except maybe black and white. As soon as we open our eyes to each new morning, we are faced with a day of choices—which side of the bed to roll out of, which body part to wash first when we shower, what to have for breakfast. As the days and years pass we make bigger choices for ourselves—where to go to school, whom to marry, how many children to have. And in between the small and the big choices are a multitude of other choices we face that influence our life and our character. Some of our choices evolve into habit and we stop thinking about them. For instance, take the first three that I mentioned: getting out of bed, showering, eating breakfast. Do you ever think about these things and make a conscious choice? Or do you slip into your habitual routine and coast on automatic pilot? Here, in the small choices we face every day, we can learn to practice awareness, acceptance, and mindfulness. Here we can begin to learn to take responsibility for ourselves. Here we can begin to understand how much of the noise in our head is there by our own choosing. As we become mindful and pay attention to each choice we make, we slowly become aware of our own investment in our difficulties. We learn how we need certain people and noises around us even though we know they interfere with our serenity. We learn how subtle some of our choices and the effects of those choices are.

If you haven't already become aware of it, notice that paradoxes are inherent in much of what is being discussed in this book. Mainly, letting go versus taking responsibility and making choices. You might be asking yourself how you can let go and make a choice at the same time. This question is appropriate and valid. But remember that without your participation in your own life you merely become an automaton. Unless you take responsibility for your choices, you will not sit squarely in your life, in the essence of who you are. This is a difficult concept to grasp, but you must make the choice, then let go, and allow your breath to enter the picture and take that choice to its natural conclusion. If you are directing the outcome, you will not be open for anything but your own narrow vision. If you ask for help and let your God in, your world will get bigger.

One thing to remember about choice is that no choice is also a choice, so if you do nothing, you are choosing to do nothing and must take responsibility for the ramifications of that choice. So review your day and think about some of the choices you made today. How many of them were made mindlessly? Can you think of one you made that you'd like to go back and change? Before you made it, did you take a moment to breathe and listen? As you breathe quietly, review your day and think about your preferred choices. What are you learning? Write about it.

We are continually faced with choices, and, luckily for us, this will never change. Some choices, of course, are more difficult to make than others. Practicing on the small ones will prepare you for the big ones. The best that you can do for yourself is to be aware of your choices and, as much as possible, the effects of each choice. Breathe deeply before deciding. Ask for guidance. Listen for the answer. And then choose. Then let go and live with the results. It will always be a perfect choice. Don't second-guess yourself. Move on to the next and the next and the next. Live fully in your life each moment. Trust your choices, and accept the results.

CRAZY CHOICES

For one week, pay attention to the small choices you are faced with and choose to do the opposite of what you'd normally do. Beginning each morning, roll out of bed on a different side. Eat before you shower, or vice versa. Eat something you don't normally eat. Take a bath instead of a shower. Wash your body from the bottom up or from the middle down. Change it each day. Continue through your day making "crazy" choices. At the end of each day, write about the day's experiences, the choices you made. How did you feel when you made them? How do you feel as you write about them? Notice anything different about yourself, about your day? What awarenesses arose? How does your body feel? Your heart? Your brain? Was it fun, or confusing and disconcerting? Why do you think you are reacting the way you are? Write about all of that. And remember to breathe deeply.

TRUST YOURSELF

For one week, take note of some of the more difficult choices you face. If a decision can wait a day, spend the evening writing and meditating on it before choosing. If not, take a few moments, go for a walk if you can, pay attention to your breath, and ask for guidance. Trust yourself. Then go back and choose. Write about it that same night, or right there and then if possible.

Carry pen and paper with you to record the things your mind and heart offer up to you during the day. If you wait until later, you may lose them. Catch them when they come, and look at them later. You might be surprised at the gems you've written. You might not recognize your own voice. Well, there it is. Start getting used to hearing it. The process is working.

6 IDENTIFY OLD HABITS AND BE WILLING TO LET SOME OF THEM GO

Good habits. Bad habits. New ones, old ones. Upon first opening our lungs and eyes as newborns, we begin to accumulate experience, learning as we go how to be functioning human beings. Layer upon layer of new knowledge is gained, and we move further and further away from being that open, vulnerable, receptive infant. We can never return to that state of innocence, nor do we want to. A clean slate is not our goal. We want to look at all that we've accumulated over the years and decide what is still of use to us and what we can discard, what we no longer want and no longer need. We may not want to clear everything away, but we could clear away the clutter and allow our minds and hearts to become open and airy, letting in light, new thoughts, and fresh air. Our true voice cannot find expression in a cluttered, stifling environment.

As a child, you may have had a special blanket or doll, or a teddy bear that you couldn't live without. Perhaps you couldn't travel or go to sleep without this treasure in your arms. It gave you a feeling of security, and you clung to it knowing that all was right with the world. You were safe and protected with it at your side. At a certain age, though, you no longer needed this object; you were able to put it behind you and move on. Maybe you replaced it with something else, intangible, in your heart or your mind. Or maybe you braved the big, scary world with no security blanket, or at least none that you could identify or put words to. More than likely, no matter how tough you were, you built up some defenses to protect yourself from harm and help yourself get along in the world. It is only natural and often necessary. But we often don't clean house as the years go by; we end up with an attic full of blankets stored in our hearts and minds. We get so stuffed to the brim we sometimes can't distinguish one blanket from another, leaving us with a noisy mess.

You've identified some of your fears and resentments and have begun to challenge yourself and let some of these go. That is a beautiful beginning. And the process continues. Think of some of the habits that you've ritualized in your life, and ask yourself some things:

- How do I approach strangers?
- How much time do I spend each week watching TV, and what are the benefits?
- Do I like to visit new places? Why or why not? How often do I do this?
- I've moved _____ times in the past ten years. What does this say about me?
- I spend _____ hours alone each week. How do I spend this time? How much enjoyment do I get from it?
- I spend no time alone. Why?

Write about all these things, and try to think of at least three more questions to ask yourself that will help identify some old, habitual ways of behaving and approaching the world. Decide for yourself what is a habit, what is a choice, what you'd like to hang on to, and what is ready to go. Then concentrate on one habit at a time and make an effort to let it go. If you no longer get enjoyment from watching TV, or if you think you'd feel better about yourself if you reduced the time spent there, or if the thought of being without TV sends you into a panic, then unhook your cable for a month and see what happens. If you are shy around strangers and immediately mistrust new people, begin to approach new people on your own, start up a conversation with the bus driver or your next waiter. Practice letting go. Practice fine-tuning your awareness, and accept yourself as you work through this process.

Sometimes we have to let go in stages. Even if our desire is strong and pure, some things just won't go away with mere wishing. But if we don't continue to try and let go little by little, these old habits will continue to cloud our hearts and minds and keep us away from our true voice. So start the process by becoming aware, move up to acceptance, and be patient with yourself. You have a lifetime of accumulated noise. It can't all disappear overnight. So breathe and be patient. You are on the right track. Remember, this is not about you being a bad person even though you're looking at your fears, your old habits. It's about taking responsibility for yourself.

EXPECTATIONS AND POSSIBILITIES

One of the side effects of moving through the world in habitual ways is that we begin to expect the world to behave as it has usually behaved. Even though we think we live in an ordered way, we are deluding ourselves. The world does not operate in any predictable fashion. So if we have expectations, we're bound to be disappointed. Even by the small things. Say you have toast every morning for breakfast and have your toaster set at medium so that each day without thinking about it you will have bread toasted to your liking. You expect that each morning your medium toast will be your breakfast. One day you go about your business as usual, habitually dropping your bread in the toaster, expecting the usual. This day it pops up much darker than you like it, nearly burnt. You forgot to check the setting. Your guest or daughter had changed it last night. Or the toaster doesn't work at all this day. You're disappointed. A simple thing. But something so simple could throw your day off. And what if there is no hot water that same morning, and the dog is sick, and it's pouring? A bad day? Could be if you expected medium toast, a healthy dog, hot water, and a sunny day. If you had no expectations, you would eat cereal, take your dog to the vet, skip a shower, and finally get to wear your new raincoat. You would be in harmony with the changing circumstances of your life.

Did you have any unfulfilled expectations today? What were they? Write about them. Do you have expectations of yourself, your life, your loved ones? What are they? Write about them. Then sit and breathe quietly as you absorb the impact of these expectations. Can you see how these might interfere with new possibilities?

Then take your lists of expectations and burn them. Let them go. Let the burning of these lists symbolize your pure intention of eliminating expectations from your life. Each time you recognize one, no matter how big or small, write it down and then burn it or visualize the burning of it in your mind. And as you do, repeat this mantra to yourself: Expect nothing—Expect nothing—Expect nothing. The surprises of the universe will then be yours. And you will live in harmony as the world about you constantly shifts and changes. You will accept all that the world brings you without resistance, without strain, and without compulsion.

Many of the exercises in this book seem simple, but if you've done any of them you already know how difficult some of them can be. Getting down to the core of you is not an easy process. It takes a lot of courage to continue the task and stay on the path, especially after difficulties arise. I want to congratulate you right now for trying. Keep it up. Trust that it gets easier. The rewards are worth it. Be kind and gentle with yourself as you progress. Remind yourself that most people are not up to this task.

Bolstering ourselves with ego-expanding behavior and activities is the current way of the world. It's odd that so many of us have huge egos juxtaposed with low self-esteem. You might wonder how this is possible, having been told that our egos directly affect the image we have of ourselves and hence our self-esteem. Big ego equals a high, healthy self-esteem. Right? Well, not exactly. As a matter of fact, the less we feed our egos and the more we practice ego deflation, the stronger our self-esteem becomes, the bigger our hearts become, and the more compassionate we become as human beings.

Although I generally don't like to use the words *good* and *bad* in their traditional meanings, I employ them here to make myself clear. Since no-ego is too difficult a concept to grasp, the ego that I refer to here is our bad-ego. There is also a good-ego, which is linked to our self-esteem and self-worth. The good-ego is supported when we are selfless, when we unconditionally care about others and seek nothing for ourselves. When we do this, we are endlessly rewarded and our good-ego is strengthened. Our bad-ego, on the other hand, serves only ourselves. We are driven by things such as pride, envy, and lust to build ourselves up and feel "good" about ourselves. Unfortunately, this often comes at the expense of others. And, as we are learning, our *Quiet Corner* aim is to keep the focus on ourselves and not react to others, to look at what we have done or could have done, to not place ourselves above or beneath anyone else. This causes our bad-ego to deflate, to become bruised, which is good. It means the process is working the way it's supposed to work. So don't be dismayed. Your good-ego will see you through.

Along with ego, we need to become familiar with humility. Because we are proud and ego driven, humility may be a foreign concept. It is not synonymous with humiliation. With humility, your good-ego is engaged. With humiliation, your bad-ego is talking to you, judging you, attacking your self-esteem, and lying to you. Being humble comes from inner strength, not weakness. Being humble quiets your bad-ego, which cannot stand up to true humility. Being humble opens your heart. In a state of humility, you can hear your inner voice more clearly. It is no longer drowned out by the loud voice of your bad-ego.

So, if some of the practices suggested here interfere with what you call your ego, then know that it's okay—know that it's more than okay, it's actually the point of some of it. Search for your good-ego so you don't feel completely abandoned. Pick up a dose of humility and carry on. Miracles will happen. You will begin to change. Your whole outlook will be different. Your inner voice will become clearer and stronger. You will begin to feel more balanced and more in harmony with yourself and your world. So crush that old ego and move forward.

YOUR OTHER HAND

Here is a simple exercise: Write one full page in your *Quiet Corner* notebook with the hand that you normally do not use. If you're ambidextrous, use your teeth to hold your pen. Write anything. Copy words from a dictionary. Perhaps you could write out the definitions of the words *ego, self-esteem, humility, humiliation,* and *pride.*

How easy is it to write with your opposite hand? How uncomfortable is it? Can you read what you've written?

This exercise accomplishes a few things. It slows us down. It gives us a new perspective on things. It helps us to appreciate the intellectual gifts and motor skills that we have. It might put us in touch with our impatience, our need to always be neat and organized, or our need to be perfect.

How does this exercise affect you? Your ego? What does it call up for you? Is humility within your reach?

Write about all this (with your "usual" hand if you'd like). And anytime you need to get in touch with some humility, repeat this exercise. Your ego may not like it, but your heart will.

THE IMPORTANCE OF
MAKING LISTS

Try to concentrate on one project or on sitting quietly and breathing. Your mind may be bombarded with all the things you have to do, people to whom you owe phone calls, what to have for lunch or dinner, what to wear to the party on Saturday, the bills you have to pay, the work you should be doing. You've dealt with many of the old voices that were taking up room in your brain, and now you're filled with new thoughts, silly thoughts, the mundane issues of your life. "What is going on here?" you might ask. "Why can't my brain just stay empty? Why must I always be thinking about something? It's too distracting, I can't sit still. I'll take care of some of these annoying chores first, then I'll sit."

A word of caution here. Your brain is very sly. It will use anything to stop you from sitting still. It will distract you from moving forward because it wants your complete attention and knows how difficult it is for you to sit still and concentrate on one thing at a time. Our brain and our subconscious are very cunning together. And they win the battle much of the time. But you can take actions to hush the voices and move on.

First, make a list of all the things you have to do so that when you're sitting, your brain can't tell you, "Don't forget about such and such." Make a list of all the people you need to get in touch with so your brain can't tell you, "Make sure you call so and so today." Once you put it on paper, it's out of your brain. You have acknowledged the need to attend to it, and your brain is empty of that issue for the moment. It will not plague you as you sit quietly. It will not interfere as you concentrate on your breath. Putting something on a list of things to do changes it at once and sometimes forever. You will find that simply writing down whatever is nagging at you will lessen its intensity immediately. It will still be important, but now you know at least that you won't forget about it. All you have to do is remember to look at your list from time to time; if you get in the habit of making lists (and we now know how easily habits are started), this will not be difficult. You might also discover that the next time you look at your list, the once nagging I-must-take-care-of-this-now issue is no longer as important as it was before you wrote it down. After a few days, you might even decide that you can ignore the issue completely. It's not so important after all.

Usually, though, the things on your list will tend to prioritize themselves after a while. If you spend time sitting and concentrating on your breath, you will intuitively know, when you return to your list, which item to address first. You might also see that your list has changed. Some things can be eliminated from your list and therefore your mind, and others will be added. Write a new list. Perhaps you can begin your day by writing a list of things to do for the day. At the end of the day, write a list of all you've done and what you think is left to do. Then compare lists and write a new one before going to bed. You will sleep better, your dreams will be richer, and your list will still be there in the morning. There's nothing to do until then. Put it on paper. Take it out of your head.

So anytime your head feels full, simply write a list and catalogue whatever's there. Write lists throughout the day. It's very satisfying to refer to these lists, scratch things off, and make new, smaller lists. This will show your progress clearly. If something never comes off your ever-changing lists, you might want to look at that a little closer. Write about what it is that's keeping you from it and why you insist on keeping it there in front of you anyway. Are you simply torturing yourself, or are you dealing with some fear around this particular issue? Maybe it's too big to be just one entry on your list. Perhaps you can break it into small chunks that might each be easier to approach. Take one small action toward this issue, chip away at it if approaching it head on and at full tilt seems too much. Try taking it off your list and see what happens. If it goes directly into your brain, creating noise, then put it back on the list. If it disappears and truly is a non-issue, great. At this point, you will be sensitive enough to know the difference. So face it or let it go. You are up to the task. And keep making lists. Their value will become apparent in no time.

KEEP IT SIMPLE

Let's try to keep our list making simple.

WORK LIST	PERSONAL LIST
1. Things to do	1. Things to do
2. People to call	2. People to call

Four lists in all. Easy. Simple. Manageable. Keep your work list at work, but if something comes up for you when you're at home, quickly write it down and then add it to your work list the following day. For those of you who work at home, this is a good way to keep the different aspects of your life separated. If your work involves tending to the kids and/or the house, it can be very easy to disregard your personal list. This system will help you to take care of your personal needs and make the separation between work and play. Keep your personal lists with you, and if something pops into your head while working, write it down for later. This way, when you're at work you can be there fully, and when you're at home you can be at home with all your attention.

DON'T THINK ABOUT ELEPHANTS

At this point in your *Quiet Corner* practice, you will have established a schedule for sitting quietly by yourself each day. If you've begun a *Quiet Corner* sharing group, you might want to extend the time you meet by twenty or thirty minutes so that you can sit quietly together concentrating on your breath. What is not so easily done alone becomes much easier with the support of a group. Have someone keep the time and be responsible for ringing a bell or softly clapping their hands when the agreed-upon time is up. That will free the rest of the group to let go, concentrate on their breath, and not be concerned with the time passing. In a group, you will notice that time seems to pass much more quickly. You will not squirm as much as when alone, and you will become aware of the power of the group, the collective energy. You will also have others with whom to share your sitting experience.

Because it isn't easy to sit still and is even more difficult to clear our heads, we cannot just say to ourselves something like this: "For the next twenty minutes or so as I sit quietly and breathe, I will empty my mind, think of nothing, and listen for my inner truth to express itself." I think if we could easily accomplish this we would be living on a planet of enlightened beings. But, unfortunately, this is not the case. We do not have such easy control over our minds. It takes time and a lot of practice just to slow our minds down. I have never discovered a way to simply not think.

The desire to "just not think" reminds me of when I was a young girl. My friends and I would sit around playing a mind game that I don't think we had a name for. We would challenge each other to not think about something. Elephants, for instance. We would sit there concentrating and straining to keep thoughts of elephants from our tiny, still-developing brains. The harder we concentrated, the more our brains would fill with elephants, until that was all we were thinking about. Elephants. It was very amusing, and although we never "won," we kept playing the game. It often ended with all of us convulsed with giggles.

The more you beg yourself to stop thinking and expect yourself to accomplish this, the more frustrated you will become and the noisier your mind will be. So rather than thinking about not thinking, just allow yourself to sit quietly and keep bringing your attention back to your breath. If a thought arises (and it will), simply try not to follow the thought to its normal conclusion. Allow that you've had a thought and then just return to your breath. Begin to count your breaths. After each full breath, count to yourself up to ten breaths and then begin again. As thoughts come to you, don't beat yourself up for thinking—just let them go, and continue counting. If you lose your count because a thought has carried you away, simply start over, bring yourself back to number one, and congratulate yourself for noticing. If you notice that you're up to breath number seventeen and you don't even know how you got there, don't worry, just bring yourself back home to the count of one on the next exhalation. And again congratulate yourself for being aware of the runaway breath counting. This is all you have to do—breathe and count, breathe and count. Don't try to stop thinking. Don't try not to think of elephants. Just concentrate on each breath. Allow your thoughts their freedom. And just breathe.

BOOK III

Taking Action

Bringing
Ourselves into
the Present

⑥ CLEAR UP THE PAST

By now you've become more aware of yourself—your fears, your
resentments, your motivations, the various voices stored in your
brain. And, if you've been taking some quiet time for yourself
each day, you've moved toward a greater acceptance of yourself,
of those you love and hate, and of the world around you. Much of
what you've done up to now has been silent and alone, except for
those times you've shared with others on the same path. Now it's
time to begin moving outward, taking action, and shifting from an
internal to more of an external housecleaning. It's time to review
your relationships again, along with any lingering resentments.
We are not talking about severing relationships. Quite the con-
trary. It's time to heal these relationships so that you can move
forward and gain some peace, experience a deeper quiet. And so
that your heart can further open to its intended purpose of love.

Begin by reviewing any troubled relationships and resentments that continue to hang on and threaten your serenity. You

must take some action to begin healing the wounds. Look at your part in the whole process. This is where you might balk and say, "But they started it . . . But if it were not for them doing . . . But if only they would have . . . But they won't even talk to me . . ." It's okay to say these things. But it's not okay to use any of them as a reason not to look at your role and clear up whatever you are responsible for. You have no control over anyone else. You never have. You never will. You cannot change the past and the things that others might have done to "cause" you to build resentment. But you can do something about your attitude toward them. You don't have to love or even like them, but this is not about them anyway, it's about you, and if you love yourself enough you will take some action toward healing the wounds.

Remember, you can do only so much. You can take care of only your half. You can be responsible only for you and your actions. If you approach these people honestly, with your head held high, and do what you can, you will notice results right away. Your negative feelings toward these people will ease, your mind will slowly become free of their grip on you, and your breath will deepen. No longer will it be blocked by anger. No longer will it get caught in your throat when you think of these people. You will breathe clearly and with no hesitation, knowing that you did all in your power to heal the relationship. You will know that the rest is up to some other power not your own. And eventually, even if some relationships don't heal completely, your heart will throb with compassion toward even the worst offenders. Your mind will be clear of the ache of resentment and will be quieter and less cluttered, ready for your true voice to find expression. So take the action to clear up your past. This will bring you into the present and make you more available to yourself and your life today.

This is a scary idea, and it's not easy. But has anything truly worthwhile ever been easy and free of fear? Think about it. Then do it. Welcome to your present life. Breathe and enjoy this moment. This is, in the end, all there is.

BEFORE AND AFTER

First, make a list of every person, place, and institution that you feel some resentment toward, even if it's minor. Be sure that anyone who has taken up residence in your brain is on this list.

Second, write a letter to each person on this list. Let it all out. Rant, rage, accuse, express your anger if you wish. And always include in each letter an admission of your own part in the drama or dance of the relationship.

Third, write a second letter to each person on your list. Do not include any reference to your anger or to their behavior. Keep it clean. Only write about your part in it.

Fourth, make arrangements to see each person on your list and talk to them about your behavior. No need to point your finger. No need to communicate your anger or resentment toward them. Chances are they already know how you feel on this score anyway. So keep the focus on yourself. Talk only of your part in the discord. If for some reason you cannot meet face to face with some of these people, then send your second letter. But always try direct contact first. Some of the people on your list may be dead or you may not know how to find some people. In these cases, write the letters and then share them with a trusted friend, with your God, and with yourself silently in your heart.

Fifth, sit quietly before and after you write each letter and before and after each encounter. Notice the before and after.

Write about each experience. Write about the before and after. Did you learn anything new about yourself?

Your mind is quieter. The voices are fewer. Your voice is stronger. A feeling of peace and contentment visits you. All is right with the world.

⑥ TAKING ACTION, LETTING GO OF RESULTS

Once you begin to take action in your life along the *Quiet Corner* path, you may find yourself clinging to the outcome, a little too invested in how it all turns out. Because such action takes a lot of courage and a strong will, you might find yourself wanting to control the result. Believing that you deserve a reward for your bravery, you might resort to old behavior and attempt to manipulate how your actions are received and what comes back to you. This is a perfect opportunity for your expectations to burst forth, so proceed with caution. It is important to be aware of this danger so as to sidestep it. Accept that you want things the way you want them and then step out of the way; take the action and let go of the result. You have been practicing letting go all along this path, and here is yet another chance to hone the skill that constantly needs sharpening.

Approach all actions the way you would bake a cake. Collecting and mixing all the ingredients, you stir them up, pour the batter into a pan, put it into the oven, and then let go of the result. You cannot climb into the oven and make sure it does its job, baking evenly and thoroughly. You have to trust that the cake will turn out. And even if one day the oven temperature is slightly off and the cake comes out somewhat overdone, it is perfect enough. There is nothing you could have done to predict or avoid the idiosyncrasies of your oven, just as you cannot predict the behavior or response of others. You can be in charge only of yourself. And if your motives are pure, your intentions are clear, and your heart is giving, all you can do is show up, take the proper action, and let go of the results. You've done your job, now let the universe do its job. Take the action. Turn it over. Let it go. Stand back. And watch how perfectly everything gets arranged. And don't forget to smile. You are allowed to enjoy this.

BEING MINDFUL

This practice of taking action and letting go of the results may seem impossible when you first begin, especially when it involves relationships and the behavior of other people. So slow down, breathe, and know that you are already practiced in this art. All you have to do is bring your mind to every activity you engage in, and you will see how experienced you already are.

For one week, pay especially close attention to—be mindful in—all your activities. "Be mindful" is another way to say "Use your purpose tool." Notice where you are and what you're doing. Involve your whole being in each activity. Concentrate fully on the matter at hand, on what is in front of you. Be aware of your breath as you move through your day. As you practice being mindful, you will notice how in so many areas that you take for granted you are already practicing the art of letting go.

Here are some examples:

- When you set your alarm at night (taking action), you sleep comfortably, trusting that it will wake you in the morning (letting go of results).
- When you turn on the water for your shower (taking action), you trust that water will come through the pipes and sprinkle down on you (letting go of results).
- When you put your tea kettle on the stove (taking action), you trust that the burner will do its job and boil your water (letting go of results).

And on and on and on throughout your day. Pay attention to the details.

Being mindful like this throughout your day, with each little and large activity, has many benefits. It will place you squarely in each moment, which is where you always want to be. It will increase your awareness and gratitude about all the simple things of life that we all so easily take for granted. It will demonstrate how you are already skilled at letting go. You will build confidence that you can take actions and let go of results in any and all areas of your life, no matter how complex or emotionally charged.

At the end of each day, write about your mindful activities. Write about instances where you weren't able to let go and why you couldn't. Don't judge yourself, just be aware for next time or the time after that. This is practice. You are not perfect. Just be mindful, breathe, and keep practicing.

Some days, you just aren't going to be up for a lot of heavy soul searching. Some days, you may feel that you can't go on, that you should just stop the whole thing. Let me remind you here that this process is difficult and that emotions are part of it. You will never be confronted with more than you can handle on any given day, you can always ask for help, and it's okay to take a break now and then and return to the process when you're ready. (If you decide to take a long break, set a date on which to return; otherwise, the old voices might take hold and keep you away forever.)

Meanwhile, lighten up! This is serious business, but there's no reason not to have a good time while you're at it. It has been proven that a sense of humor and laughter can be both emotionally therapeutic and physically healing. Besides that, it just plain feels good to laugh. Have you ever laughed so hard you cried, after which an enriching calm enveloped you? When was the last time you felt this? Do you think you have a sense of humor? Do you like to laugh? Are you drawn to people who laugh a lot? When you laugh, can you feel the benefits immediately? Our mind calms down, our body relaxes, our point of view shifts when we laugh, so it is important to keep your sense of humor intact and laugh often. When you feel your heart getting heavy or your mind talking at you, take a break, let it all go, put everything on the shelf, and have some fun. There's no need nor any benefit to sitting in a pool of self-pity. So drag yourself out, laugh at yourself, and move away from that trap. Remind yourself that you can walk away for a while, get some fresh air, and come back to it anytime you choose. And know that after you walk away and lighten up a little, you will return with a lighter heart. Everything will look and feel different.

There is also no reason not to lighten up even when you're in the thick of it. In fact, there's every reason to lighten up. And it's possible to do this without walking away and changing course. Simply shift your perspective in the very moment that you notice yourself taking it all too seriously. Simply close your eyes. Take three deep, three-part breaths. Move your facial muscles into a smile even if you must use your fingers to make it happen. Think of the last thing that made you laugh. Focus on that for a moment and laugh out loud if you can, at the memory. Your body will remember how to laugh even if your brain resists. So give yourself over to your body and overpower that mind resistance with good, old-fashioned laughter.

At times, this laughter might turn to tears. That's okay too. Maybe you need a good cleansing cry. This also helps us to lighten up, to release the tension, and to make us feel freer. So go for it. Breathe, smile, cry, and laugh. And enjoy learning about yourself. You don't have to wait until you're so deep in the depths of seriousness that you have to walk away. Remember that the point of this whole process is to find out what you really want in life so that you can be happier and experience more joy in life. Soon the heaviness will disappear completely or appear less often, and you will be light of heart and mind. Put in the hard work, experience the pain and joy of the process, and lighten up. Delight in the small epiphanies and breakthroughs—feel the weight of the world roll off your back—and you might even experience moments of floating on air.

YOUR FUNNY BONE

Laughter can be contagious. If you have a hard time conjuring up a smile or a belly laugh, make a point of seeking out someone who can make you laugh. A funny friend, a funny movie. You know best about your own funny bone and what tickles it. Children are always a good source for laughter. If you don't have children of your own, visit a friend or relative who has small children, or take a trip to your neighborhood playground or local zoo. Children can sometimes take themselves very seriously, but do you ever notice how quickly they can be coaxed out of that mood and how once they're laughing they seem to forget ever being in it? We all had this facility at one point in our lives, but the worries of adulthood contributed to our losing it. It is this easy, light mood that we want to return to. So visit some children and learn from them. Learn to tap into your own childish funny bone.

After spending some time with children paying specific attention to how they enjoy themselves, write about the experience. What did you learn? What can you begin to do to recapture your child-spirit? What can you introduce into your daily life to remind yourself to lighten up?

⑥ THE ANSWERS ARE IN
THE SILENCE

It is so easy to get caught in the trap of intellectualization. We believe that we can think our way through anything, that we can figure it all out intellectually. And this stance will often convince us that we can skip the one part of this process that initially seems most unnatural, the part that is probably the most difficult, the part of being quiet and sitting still.

Yet this is the one part that cannot be skipped. This is the part to which we bring all the others for synthesis. This is where we learn that some questions are not answered intellectually. This is where we learn to trust a deeper truth, where we make sense of all the rest, even though we may never have the words to attach to this understanding.

Learning this takes some time, especially for people who are new to meditation. So, whenever confusion or fear visit, go to the silence. Whenever, always, every day, visit this silent place, this place inside you, and you will know. Just sit still, breathe, and listen. Soon you'll find it easier to make decisions. You'll instinctively begin to know what to do and what is right for you. The answers are there, waiting to be heard. So go there, and wait and trust that all you need to know is in the silence. All the answers are there. In the silence.

8

Settling into the Everyday

⑥ BALANCE

As you continue on your *Quiet Corner* path, you will notice that you become disturbed less easily, that you have more patience for others, that the noise in your head has calmed down, and that you are not so readily distracted by other people. You will also be more aware of your own behavior and its effect on others. You will be more careful with your criticisms of yourself and others, and you will be more aware of your fear and yet less afraid than ever. You will know more clearly what you want and be more able to let go of your desires. And you will learn to be grateful for all that you have. Emotional and spiritual balance will be yours, creating harmony in all areas of your life.

All this may sound unobtainable and a bit too grand. But I promise that if you do the work, if you make the effort, if you are sincere in your desire to seek spiritual fulfillment, then a balanced life will be yours. For example, as you get better at putting yourself right where you are and living in each moment, you will become more efficient and productive at work, which will free you up to spend more time with friends and family or with a hobby. As you own up to your part in all relationships, you will become less irritable and less prone to strike out or snap at people, whether they're intimates or strangers. As you see yourself more clearly, you will have more tolerance for the idiosyncrasies of others. As you learn to stop, breathe, and center yourself whenever one of your warning bells goes off, your level of stress will be much reduced. You will turn from a horn blowing, accusation throwing, aggressive driver into someone who takes advantage of the standing time at a red light, who gives others the right of way, who reaches his or her destination on time—calm and ready for the next challenge.

All your problems are not going to disappear, but you will begin to see them as challenges and be less overwhelmed by them. You will even become aware that some of the stress in your life is self-induced and that you have some control over it, that you have more choices than you were ever aware of. You might even miss the "excitement" of your old life, that jampacked-never-have-enough-time-what-will-I-do-next kind of life.

Once your life changes into a less hectic, more balanced, time-will-reveal-all kind of life, you might want to retreat back into your old ways for a while. This is a perfectly normal reaction. We are often more comfortable in our familiar pain than in unfamiliar serenity. So revisit your old self for a while if you must. Continue to go back and forth until you're used to your new self and can live with it comfortably on a daily basis. At some point, the old pain will become tiresome and you will no longer have a need for it. And then you will be in balance, you will stroll down the path of the middle way, and you will know that you exist in the truth of yourself. You will be a beacon of light, guiding others along the path, clear and luminous in your intensity. Welcome to the wonderful world that we were all meant to live in.

AN ATTITUDE OF GRATITUDE

Sometimes when we reach a point of balance in our lives, we don't always know it. Since all this is a very slow process, we can't always notice how far we've come. Sometimes we may even feel that nothing has changed, causing us to slip into a self-indulgent state of dissatisfaction. This is a perfect time to write a gratitude list. You might even want to include this in your daily writing practice. This simple act can extinguish your negativity immediately. And it can prevent it from appearing at all if you write a daily list. So write about those small things that you are grateful for—the sun streaming in your bedroom window, the candleholders on your mantel, your flannel sheets. Then the big things—the love of your partner or child or friend, the food on your table, the ability to read and write. This exercise will introduce a little humility into your day and help to quiet any fear that you don't have enough or that you might lose what you do have. Keep it simple. Write the list. Don't think too much. Just be grateful. That is enough.

⑥ DON'T COMPARE

As you progress along the *Quiet Corner* path, you don't always see your own progress, especially when your mind takes you hostage. It becomes important then to associate with people who are on a similar path or to find a spiritual mentor, someone you admire. It is often easier to see your own growth in someone else, so using others as a mirror into yourself can be useful. But be careful not to compare yourself. See yourself and your progress through others, but don't compare. Just know that you are moving and growing along your own unique path in your own unique way, as they are moving along theirs, and that your progress won't compare exactly with anyone else's. If you can keep the focus on yourself, using others only as a barometer, then you have truly come a long way on this path in trusting yourself and allowing your own unique voice to find expression.

One common trap that many of us fall into as we begin to take measure of ourselves is that of comparing our insides with someone else's outsides. As you get more in touch with your true nature and allow your inner voice to express itself no matter what, there may be days when you feel torn apart inside, days when you feel especially vulnerable, or days when your old judge and critic return to torment you. When you look out at the world in this fragile state you might be tempted to compare how you're feeling inside with how others appear to be feeling as you look at their outsides. Remember that our outsides are not always a true reflection of what's going on in our depths. Chances are, even when you are in an emotionally vulnerable state, you continue to project your usual self to the world. Your outsides do not always accurately reflect your insides, and the same can be said for everyone else. Remind yourself that you really don't know how the object of your comparison is really feeling. You can only know that whatever you are feeling will pass and that these feelings are just the momentary you, not the permanent you.

When we are unaccepting of our emotional state and want to move out of it into a new and different state, we might look at others and interpret what we see to suit our need. We might look at others and see them all as happy and content, placing our own discontented mood in stark contrast. Then the internal whining and questioning begins, as we focus on what we think they have and what we seem to be lacking. This is where you need to ask yourself, "How do I know they're so happy? How do I know they don't feel as bad as I do?" When you look at others and compare, you are taking the focus off yourself and your feelings. This probably means there is something going on inside you that you don't want to look at. This comparing with others is dangerous and just another voice in your head that you need to let go of.

Often this comparing syndrome begins with the externals and gives us a sense of not being enough. Then this feeling of not being enough works its way inside and we begin to believe it. Then we take those feelings and think that they are us, that we are only those feelings. We think that everyone can see how awful and different we are. Then we look at others and see the outside, thinking that it reflects the inside because by now we feel turned inside out and believe that they can see our feelings. Our habit of comparing kicks in, and we end up comparing apples and oranges without knowing it. Then we are just a bundle of feelings. Everyone who crosses our path looks happy and secure within themselves.

This is when it's time to put on the brakes. Employ your purpose tool. Ground yourself in the now. Take a reality check. Stop for a moment and see where you are and what you're doing, before you get carried away and spiral into self-pity. Breathing is the first step. Move your attention away from the apples versus oranges and toward your breathing. Take a walk, notice where you are, look at things and not other people, drink in the beauty around you. Then once you've found your breath, your center, write about whatever is going on inside. Make a phone call to someone who can help you work through it. Write about how it all started, about what you might be avoiding, about your feelings then and now. Don't judge yourself for the behavior. We all do it. Realize as you come back to yourself with heightened awareness that you are different from all those people you compared yourself with. Different. Not better, not worse, just different. Accept this about yourself as you would accept it about someone else. Be as generous with yourself as you would be with someone else.

If you walk around always looking at others, focused on their place, and comparing yourself, your attention is outside and far away from your own inner voice. Continue to draw yourself back to *your* center, back to *your* voice, back to *your* breath. Be yourself. Stop trying to be someone else.

A SELF-PORTRAIT

Write about all the things that make you you. Write about your quirks, your idiosyncrasies, your likes and dislikes, your passions, habits, and hobbies. Then list your physical qualities. Don't qualify or judge, just describe them.

Now write a funny story about this person you've detailed using as many of the specifics as possible. Write it as though this person were a stranger whom you were just getting to know. Don't think. Just write for twenty minutes. Have fun!

At the end of twenty minutes, do you find yourself liking this person? Did he or she make you laugh or cry? Can you see yourself in this person? Can you see yourself now as likeable?

Now draw a portrait of this person. Even if you can't draw. This is only for fun, to exercise your right brain, to take you away from your thinking mind. Use crayons or watercolors or just a black pen. Put this person in a scene that fits with the qualities you detailed.

Did you learn anything new about yourself after doing these exercises? Write about that. Do you know yourself any better? Write about that.

A woman I know attended a weekend retreat last year at a Zen Buddhist monastery in the Catskill Mountains of New York. She was introduced to meditation, attended yoga classes, and renewed her enjoyment of this practice. She met a group of like-minded people, and then returned to the city refreshed and rejuvenated, ready to repeat the experience. She couldn't wait to go back.

The sense of peace and the overall feeling of well-being that she came home with left her after a few days, so she started to incorporate yoga and meditation into her life to achieve harmony on a more consistent basis. The feeling she had after the weekend never quite returned, although she continued to want it and half-heartedly pursued it.

It seems that she had experienced something that weekend that made her want to change her life. But at the next opportunity presented to her to return to the mountains, she resisted. Her mind settled on what she thought she didn't like about the week-end. She didn't want to drive for three hours there and back in a car with three or four strangers. She started to complain about how cold the mountain air was, how she had never felt warm. The shared bathroom and shower facilities were not to her liking, and she didn't want to subject herself to such deprivation again. She decided not to attend another retreat. The sense of well-being that she had experienced did not outweigh the negatives in her mind. She will probably never return to the place that had given her a new outlook on life. She said that if she could only have that feeling again she'd be so happy. But she wasn't willing to do what it took to get it.

This attitude is not so unusual. Although we may often want peace of mind and a serene heart, we don't always want to take the steps to reach them. We start *thinking* about the process and the pain involved. We exaggerate in our minds the small inconveniences that are inherent in the process and build them up to being major roadblocks. We create a road in our mind littered with obstructions, so we turn the other way, convinced that we have no choice. But this is just us getting in our own way.

Once you've done your internal housecleaning and rid your mind of some of the voices that don't belong to you, you may find that your days pass peacefully enough with less mind clutter than ever but that you easily become distracted from spending *Quiet Corner* time alone. You start getting in your own way. You become an obstacle to yourself as you spend too much time thinking about where you're going. No longer can you blame your parents or boss or spouse. No longer can you justify procrastination. No longer can you avoid quiet listening with a clear conscience. Yet you still resist it. This resistance is your ego-mind working against you. This is quite normal. Don't beat yourself up. Just accept it, don't give in to it, and move on.

Some of the ways that we get in our own way can be quite subtle. We may not even know that we are impeding our own progress. Do you ever wish your time away? Can't wait for the evening, day, event, to end? This is a sign that you are not sitting in the present, squarely in your center. When you find yourself in such a state, simply start your day over. Right then. As soon as you take notice. At that moment. And you'll swing back to center instead of off into the stratosphere.

Though there is much value to daydreaming and living in our imagination, we sometimes get caught in the un-reality trap, where we spend more and more time each day wishing and hoping, dreaming, fantasizing, and wanting. Too much time spent here can be dangerous and can remove us so far from reality that our true nature and inner voice become lost in the mire. If you become aware of such a tendency, take an action before you are too far gone. Bring yourself into the present by moving your body and paying attention to each step you take. Ground your awareness into the bottom of your feet. Or open your notebook and describe the scene directly in front of you. Taking an action will ground you and introduce some perspective into your world. This also works if you find yourself spinning off into a fear mode. Taking an action will usually drive the fear away and illustrate how your fear was not grounded in reality in the first place. Sometimes, just speaking the fear out loud to someone else is action enough and will begin the process of dissipating the fear.

Once we push through all the barriers that we construct for ourselves to keep us from ourselves, there are often even more once we get to our quiet place. All the barriers we put up before we get there and when we're there come from our minds, our egos, our fears. Our mind tells us that we have more pressing things to do. Our ego tells us that there's no satisfaction in going inward, that we need to pay more attention to how we look and to what others think of us. Our fear keeps us stuck in limbo because it wants to know what's going to happen or what we'll find— before it happens and before we see it.

Be brave and know that you are not just your mind-ego-fear obstacles. You are much more than that. You are your heart. You are your belly. You are your breath. You are your true voice. You are your God. When you learn to recognize how you get in your own way and then learn to get out of your own way, you will move ever closer to yourself.

THE WALLS WE BUILD

Write a list of all the ways you think you get in your own way. Think in terms of your relationships, your job, your art or hobbies, your spiritual path.

For one week, pay attention to how you get in your own way. Anytime you feel up against a wall, consider the possibility that you put it there, even if this is not immediately apparent. Until you write about it, you may not be aware of your contribution to it. So open your eyes, open your heart, and write about your day-to-day impediments.

⑥ BLOCKS CAN BE
USED TO BUILD

Pushing through the barriers we construct for ourselves is important to moving on toward our true selves. But there is often much to learn about our true nature if we stop for just a moment and take a look at what's blocking us. Rather than jump over the barriers, stop and rip them down brick by brick. These bricks can then be used to pave your road. If we never stop and always just push things out of our way (though at times this is appropriate), we will never learn why these blocks are there in the first place. And they will keep cropping up.

So each time you hit a block, stop and take a look. Examine it, talk about it, write about it, pray about it, and sit quietly with it in front of you. Gradually, it will begin to erode, to make sense. Gradually you will learn a new thing about yourself. Your inner voice will rise from the rubble you've made of this barrier.

My friend Leslie (who had been procrastinating about her taxes) learned a valuable lesson from the huge barrier she constructed for herself. Since she works on a free-lance basis, her income can fluctuate quite radically. This year, the work has not been all that plentiful. Her fear of not having enough money spilled over into all areas of her life. She was afraid that she hadn't paid enough taxes last year, and since she wasn't making much money and felt she couldn't afford to pay more than she already had, she put off filing. She lived with a heap of tax papers that needed organizing and always found a reason not to tackle it. She lived with economic insecurity and was withholding in all her relationships as a result. Often angry, she found many reasons to justify her feeling, ignoring the abscess that had become her unfiled taxes. She lived with this situation for six months, and her life became completely unmanageable. She had trouble focusing on her work, making decisions, dealing with her daughter. And the mess on her desk began to spread throughout her apartment, until she found herself living in chaos.

After talking about it to friends and writing and praying about it, Leslie began to take action. One small action after the other, one day at a time, she eventually filed her taxes, hoping for the best. When told that she had overpaid by $5,000, she was speechless, grateful, and humble. With this behind her, Leslie's heart is now much lighter, and she no longer suffers from lack of work. This has been a powerful lesson for Leslie and will remain in her consciousness for many years, teaching her about fear and procrastination. Maybe the next time she's confronted with a roadblock or a bundle of fear, the lesson she learned here will help her avoid more unnecessary suffering.

A risk not taken is an opportunity missed. Most of us would like to know the outcome of any choice or decision we make before we make it. We want to know the future. We read tarot cards, consult psychics, have our palms read, or look for our daily horoscope to know what lies ahead of us. Playing it safe is a way of life for some of us. We think we would be happier if we could know the future. We'd even be happy to know *some* of it, just the repercussions of this choice or the rewards or pitfalls of that one.

But we can't know our future, so our job is to arrive at some peace with the unknowing. Some things, of course, we can be reasonably sure of, and this little bit of knowledge often confuses us and deludes us into thinking that more must be knowable. So we sit and wait for the future to speak to us, and before we know it we are in the future. Whatever choice we were grappling with was either made for us or has become irrelevant and we are on to the next. This is avoidance living, and many of us do it.

When you wake up each morning, consider that everything you do, every choice you make, is a risk. Then, all risks will become equal, surprise will await you at every turn, and you will no longer concern yourself with the future. Simply place yourself in each moment, moving to the next only when it arrives. This is not to say that you should walk through your life like a zombie, unprepared and foolishly naive. You should try to walk through your life in a state of awareness and heightened anticipation. Walking across a busy street is as much a risk to some of us as quitting our jobs and pursuing our dreams is to others. The first only seems less risky because we may do it so often. So if we begin to take bigger risks in our life more often, they too will become easier.

My aunt Ruth was close to eighty when she, my aunt Edna, and my mother came to visit me in New York City. I escorted them to a holiday show at Radio City Music Hall in midtown. When Aunt Ruth was confronted with crossing the Avenue of the Americas, she was quite timid and a little scared. She came from a small town in Rhode Island, and all the streets she had to cross in her life were quite negotiable. But this huge, busy, noisy, crowded avenue in New York was quite another matter. I, on the other hand, never gave it much thought, often crossing against the light if there was time, as most experienced New Yorkers do. As I led the way across the street, the Don't Walk sign started flashing and I kept walking, knowing that we had enough time to cross before the traffic began to move. But my aunt refused to leave the curb. So we waited for the green, Ruth holding onto my arm for dear life, and then proceeded on our way. Aunt Ruth enjoyed the show but was happiest when she was aboard the bus that would take her back home, where she knew how to cross the streets.

Crossing the Avenue of the Americas was a genuine risk for my aunt. She never returned to New York, but if she had spent more time here crossing the streets, the risk factor eventually would have subsided and she might have ended up wondering why it once scared her so. Yet it remains that it is risky to cross the busy streets of Manhattan. But New Yorkers do it anyway, forgetting the risk. This is how we should approach anything that seems like a risk, especially if we know that fear is the only thing holding us back. Do it anyway. Chances are you will make it to the other side of the street. And even if the trip is fraught with fear, it is better than standing on the curb stuck in fear, paralyzed, wondering what it would be like to cross, wishing that you had the courage.

As you go through each day, become aware of all the small risks you take and the ones you avoid taking. If you have some indecision, waiting for the future to be foretold, go to your *Quiet Corner* and sit on it. By now you will be closer in touch with your inner voice—and this, rather than some fortune teller, is where you need to go. Your inner voice may not be able to tell the future, but it will let you know in which direction to move. It will help you either to put aside the question at hand or to move forward, take the risk, and deal with the fear. Your true self will always be there, supporting you and guiding you. And each time you take a risk, with your inner voice as guide, you will build up your risk-taking experience so that next time will be easier. Before you know it, other people will be lauding you on your bravery while you simply take it in stride, one precious moment at a time.

CONCENTRATION

For one week, pay attention to the small risks you take and those that you avoid. Write about them at the end of each day. Observe your behavior and your state of mindfulness each time. How present are you in each circumstance? Are you more present for one than for another? Which makes you feel better about yourself? Whose voice decides for you what is risky and what isn't?

Some years ago on TV was a game show called "Concentration." Contestants were asked questions, and a correct answer would reveal a letter to a phrase or sentence that was hidden behind a large wall panel. For each correct answer, a square with a letter on it would be turned over to reveal yet more of the puzzle. As more was revealed, the contestants would try their luck at deciphering the clues. The first to guess would win the prize. My friend Steve, who is in a twelve-step recovery program, recently described to me how this game reminded him of his life. He says that he continues to get clues about himself and is closer to putting together the mystery of his life each day he shows up for it.

Think of your inner voice as this "Concentration" board. Each of the suggested exercises here will turn over a square and reveal one more thing about you and your true nature. Each exercise will give you a clue to deciphering who you really are and what your inner voice wants to tell you.

So write about the risks you take and don't take, and more will be revealed. More of the blank space will be filled in. Concentrate on your life, and the answers to your most perplexing questions will be answered. The prize will be yours.

TAKE A CHANCE

Write about all the big risks you feel you've taken in your life and the repercussions of those risks. Then write about all the times you played it safe, avoiding the risks, and the repercussions of those actions.

Then write about one decision you are faced with today (start with something small), about the safe approach and then the risky approach. Write the pros and cons for each. If you know exactly where the safe approach will lead you, then just this once, choose what you think is the risky way. Take a chance. Be courageous. Because you are.

Whenever you know them, write about the repercussions of that choice.

Keep experimenting with small risks and build up some risk-taking experience. Then move on to the larger issues in your life. Consult with your inner self. You will be exhilarated and know that you are fully alive. Scary, yes. But, oh, so worth it!

Surely you've heard the phrase "Change is inevitable." And surely you've not only experienced this but deep in your gut you know the true simplicity of it. So why do so many of us expect the status quo to remain the status quo? Why does the least little thing that we weren't expecting sometimes throw us off course? And why can't we simply accept change as easily as we accept the routine, even when we know that routine can be boring and change can be exciting? Even when change often carries with it new and surprising results that we on our own would never have imagined? Even when these changes make our lives sweeter and more interesting and make us feel more alive?

I believe that we resist change because we sit in our private worlds stuck in self-centered fear, thinking that the world has nothing to do with us, and vice versa. We think we are in charge of our own, tiny, ego-driven universe. Once we start on the *Quiet Corner* path, this bubble of delusion gets punctured. We begin to see through the haze that we once thought protected us and notice that there is life beyond this bubble, that we are all indeed connected to each other and to our collective life force. The world is sunnier and friendlier and less scary than we imagined.

Have you ever planned a picnic, been rained out, and improvised a sheltered day playing cards instead of softball? Toasting marshmallows over the gas range? Or have you ever had a flat tire that led to an unforgettable experience with a stranger and a strange town? Somehow, big events that we know are truly out of our control—such as weather changes and flat tires—we can accept unconditionally. Sure, we might be disappointed, and we may get in a bad mood because things aren't happening when and how we want them to. But we know that there is nothing we can do. It is completely out of our hands. We are not in charge. Yet the vicissitudes and vagaries of everyday life are often not so easily accepted.

If we accept these rules and apply them in our daily lives, our sail through life may not be less bumpy, but it will be thrilling and a lot more fun. Probably our most memorable life experiences are the result of something going awry. If everything always went our way and there were no sudden and unexpected surprises, how boring life would be. Unpredictability is where the joy is. Getting lost on the back roads of a strange place forces you to stop at a gas station to ask directions. You are not only lost, but irritable and hungry. Turns out there's a diner behind the gas station, so you decide to eat and are treated to the best home-cooked meal you ever tasted. Or, by not getting the promotion at work that you wanted, you are sent to Chicago on a business trip where you meet your future spouse.

If you are having trouble accepting certain changes that happen in your life, go to your *Quiet Corner* and consult with your inner self. Find out where the joy is. Go through the change (since you probably have no choice anyway), and open up to the miracle that waits for you on the other side. Let your inner voice comfort you and show you the way. Trust that you will be taken care of and that such changes are not imposed upon you to make your life miserable. Embrace the change, and it will serve you. Resist it, and accept the misery of that choice. Change is inevitable and mostly out of your control, but how you handle it is within your control. It's your life—you decide.

ADDING SPICE

Write about some past events that were transformed from the way you first imagined them as a result of changing circumstances that were beyond your control. How did you handle the change?

What was the outcome? Compare your vision with the reality. What did you expect to happen, and what actually happened? Does hindsight give you any perspective? Were there unexpected and wonderful gifts that would not have been forthcoming in your scenario? What were they?

Review in your mind the past week, and write about some changes that you were faced with that you had not counted on. How did you handle them? Did you go with the flow, or resist and try to force your will? If you resisted, imagine what would have happened had you not, and write about that. If you embraced the change and went with it, imagine if you had not, and write about that. Probably you have both types of experiences in your history. Look at both sides and decide where you would prefer to be. Decide which side of change suits you and nurtures your inner peace. Listen to your inner voice each time and trust your instincts. Even when you see it coming, change can be discomfiting. But come it will, and you may as well open your heart to it than turn your back. It's easier that way, and you'll find it more in sync with the real you. You can handle it. You can even use it to your advantage. You may even learn to love it. If nothing else, you'll surely agree that it adds spice to an otherwise bland life. So give thanks tonight and every night that you're not in charge. Give thanks each time for the discomfort that change brings. Embrace change, and it will embrace you.

⑥ SITTING STILL, THINKING ABOUT ELEPHANTS

We've seen how nearly impossible it is to will our minds to stop thinking and to move away from some idea or image that has been introduced to it. Like elephants. So let's use this proclivity we have to our advantage.

The next time you retreat to your *Quiet Corner* for a session of sitting still and concentrating on your breath, bring thoughts of elephants with you. As you slow down and begin to concentrate on your breath, bring your breath even deeper than usual. Put your breath in the center of your belly. Then imagine a hammock or saucer in your belly that extends from your navel to your tailbone. As you inhale, swing your breath to your navel, filling up your belly. As you exhale, slide your breath along the hammock and release your breath out your tailbone. Keep your breath in the hammock and gently breathe. As you develop a rhythm, think about the word *elephant* each time you exhale. Slowly, as you continue to do this, begin to drop letters off the end of the word. When you're ready, exhale *elephan*. Then exhale *elepha*. Then *eleph*. Until you are left with just the first two letters, *el*. Keep imagining your breath in the hammock. Inhale, fill your belly. Exhale out your tailbone, *el*. Keep your breath there for the remainder of your sit—five, ten, twenty, thirty minutes.

You may not be able to think only of elephants the first, second, or third time you try this. Other thoughts will rise up. Let them. But don't chase them. This is when your inner voice will also want to have its say. If you're off chasing a thought, you won't be available to hear your inner voice. So, as much as possible—and you won't be perfect—just breathe and don't think about anything but elephants.

When your true voice speaks, you may not know it to be your true voice right away. You may be far away from your *Quiet*

Corner sitting practice when you have one of those aha! experiences where you recognize your inner voice—you notice some clear truth rising up spontaneously into your consciousness. Either you will remember something that rose up during a session or you will hear it for the first time after the session. But you will know. Don't be fooled into thinking that sitting isn't necessary if you never hear your inner voice while there. It is the concentration that you practice there, the breathing that you do there, and the sitting still and listening that carry over into your everyday life that make you ready to hear. So practice listening in your *Quiet Corner* and you will learn to hear wherever you are, whenever your inner voice cares to express itself. From elephants to inner truth.

9

Staying in the Present

BE IN YOUR LIFE

One day my good friend Tom was looking at an outline for this book, saw the title of this chapter, and said, "That. That is what I need to learn how to do. It seems I'm never in my life. I don't know whose life I'm in, but it's not mine. Can you teach me how to be in my life?"

Indeed, for most of his adult life Tom has been in a job he hates, simply because he is stuck, constantly lured by the money he makes, never sure what he wants to do. So he spends forty to fifty hours a week not being himself. For years I've listened to Tom complain about his job. I've watched him as he struggled with the issue of what to do with his life. He would quit his job for periods of time and return to school, thinking that it would carry him away from his past and into a new future. He loved school but didn't enter a program that would guarantee employment. Instead, he pursued a course of study that was close to his heart, American history. This was not an error in judgment, it was his desperate attempt to get in touch with his true self. No other choice at those times would have been suitable. But each time he began to run out of money he would return to his old job. He felt trapped by the good money he made even though he was financially responsible for no one but himself. At times he seriously contemplated moving away from New York, convincing himself that it was time, but both of us knew it was just a ploy to extricate himself from his dreaded job. Life went on, the years passed, and Tom, no matter how much time he spent thinking about it, was no closer to being in his life.

Tom and I became friends about twelve years ago because of our mutual interest in books. I was working in a bookstore at the time, and he and I would often talk about opening our own store. But Tom was attached to the good money he was making serving food and drinks at one of the oldest pubs in the city. He saw how hard it was for me to live on my meager income and was just not ready to make the sacrifice. He always had some reason to keep his job, something he needed the money for. As is usual for people in their twenties and early thirties, Tom figured he had time. It would all work out in time. He had his whole life ahead of him.

We never opened our bookstore. My life took off in a different direction. Tom stayed put, making money and pouring drinks. It seems he was living for the day his life would change. He was living for the future, where anything could happen. He was biding his time knowing that anything is possible. For most of those years Tom had no clue that he wasn't in his life. Now that Tom is in his forties, he is suddenly waking to this fact. For years he believed he was living in the moment and that the future would take care of itself. But in reality he was living in the future, divorced from himself and his present state of mind. Time passed, nothing much changed, and he lived with an underlying feeling of discontent and a gnawing sense of emptiness. He was always wanting out. And he wasn't aware of what to do. Every time he looked at his life, it seemed that he had fallen deeper and deeper into the rut.

There is nothing inherently wrong with making a living serving people food and drinks. The tragedy in Tom's case is that he never wanted to be at work doing what he was being paid to do. Perhaps if he had been there at his job—body, mind, heart, soul, and spirit—things would have changed for him. He either would have begun enjoying his job or would have made a change to something else long ago. Instead, fear kept him stuck in one place, as though his feet were planted in cement. Being in the present does not mean being stuck and unable to move.

So, no matter what you're doing—for a living or for play—if you are there for it—in body, mind, heart, soul, and spirit—you can't be anywhere else. You can't be in the past, mourning your bad fortune or waxing nostalgic over the good times. You can't be in the future, dreaming of what's next, of the possibilities of your life, and wishing time away. People who live in the past and future suddenly wake up at middle age and ask themselves, "How did I get here?" Or they have a midlife crisis because they've been on automatic pilot for years, not living.

So, each day, try not to judge where you go, just go there and be there. If you use this approach, everything will take care of itself. With your feet planted in the present moment, you will gain a new respect for your life. You will not be distracted by thoughts of what has already happened or what might happen, and you will be open and available to hearing what your true voice wants to say to you. If you are meant to change where you are in your life, by remaining in the present you will have the courage to make a move. If you are meant to continue on as you are, you will have a fuller appreciation of your whole life. So change where you are or stay put—it makes no difference. Simply be there for whatever it is your life offers up to you. And you will be more alive. That sense of emptiness will disappear, and you will be in your life.

ARE YOU IN YOUR LIFE?

How would you respond to the following?

- ☙ I misplace my keys _____ times a day/week/month.
- ☙ I always know where I put my keys.
- ☙ I sometimes have a better time preparing for vacation, and then afterward showing pictures from it, than actually being on vacation.
- ☙ I often think about what I should or shouldn't have done.
- ☙ I spend a lot of time thinking about what I could and should and want to do in the future.
- ☙ If I find myself with some unexpected free time, I am at a loss.
- ☙ I often overcommit myself and find that I can't say no.
- ☙ I am too busy to worry about whether I'm in my life or like what I do.
- ☙ I live for the weekends.
- ☙ I get depressed on the weekends.
- ☙ I often work late and on the weekends.
- ☙ I always look forward to going back to work on Sunday night.
- ☙ My Sunday nights are awful because I dread going back to work on Monday.

Write about these and just let your pen flow. Whatever comes up for you around these issues, write about it. Then put it aside and sit quietly with yourself for a while. Breathe into your belly and notice what's there. Has anything been stirred up? Have you made peace with a previously burning issue? What is your inner voice saying to you about your place in your life?

CROSSING THE BORDER

I visited New Mexico for the first time about ten years ago, and since then I have been constantly drawn back. Although I once thought I would not like the desert, I now consider it a very spiritual place. So familiar with the green and wet of New England, I thought that the desert would be lifeless and monotonous. Instead, I found it teeming with life and explosions of color and quiet. I am always astounded by its beauty and respond viscerally to its power, which affects my emotional and creative moods in a very positive way.

During a recent trip there, I became intensely aware of New Mexico's profound effect on me. I entered from the north after driving through Colorado and having a terrific time. I didn't notice crossing the border until I became aware of a sharp change in my mood. I had been enjoying the scenery, but at a certain point it was as though I was seeing with every part of my body and mind. My eyes took what they saw and sent waves of pleasure to my heart, my belly, my mind, my feet, my brain, my fingertips. I was absorbed into the landscape and it coursed through me. I didn't think about what I was seeing—I just saw it. My right brain became ultra-alert and creatively stimulated. While this may sound like a mystical experience, I was clearly and surely grounded on this planet in the desert of New Mexico. I will never forget that experience, and I think of it often when I feel myself not appreciating my life. Being in the past or the future is the first clue that I'm not in my present life. So I bring myself in my mind to the border of New Mexico and cross over into the here and now, into a wakeful and alert state. The memory of New Mexico lives in my body, so I don't always have to be physically there to swim in its magnificence. I simply let it live in my right brain where it is always available to me . . . reminding me of the gifts that come with living in the moment. I simply recall the border experience each time I feel stuck, each time I become aware that I'm thinking too much, each time I want to loosen my creative juices, each time I realize that I'm not living in the present. I imagine that the left side of my brain (the side that controls verbal, analytic, and thought processes) is Colorado, and the right side of my brain (the side that controls nonverbal, spatial, and perceptual processes) is New Mexico. I then cross the border of my mind and step into my creative center.

Think of a place, a thing, or a person particularly meaningful to you—one that brings you unconditional joy or serenity. A few suggestions: God, a waterfall, Mother Teresa, breath, the ocean, the Milky Way, Gandhi, a rose, a mountaintop. First let go of any feelings you might have about not being in that place or with that person. Let go of the need to be there in the flesh. Don't choose a place or someone that you have an unhealthy attachment to. Then put this person, thing, or place into your right brain, the side of your brain where your creativity resides, your nonrational, nonlogical activity. Let this person or place represent your awareness, your pure intention, your inspiration.

Every time you find yourself residing too much in your left brain—thinking, thinking, thinking—cross the border into your right brain and visit your inspiration. Every time you find yourself drifting back into the past or forward into the future, cross the border of your mind. Every time you need to be reminded of your potential, of where and who you are, visit your right brain and put yourself back in your life, back in the present moment where everything and anything is possible. No need to move. No need to go someplace else. No need to change your circumstances. Just close your eyes, breathe, and cross the border of your mind. Then enter the limitless and bountiful present. Give yourself the present of your own presence. Right here. Right now. This moment.

Until I started my sitting practice, I didn't understand why some people would intentionally place themselves in dangerous situations—jumping out of airplanes, climbing steep mountains, driving superfast cars. But after many years of simply sitting quietly and concentrating on my breath, in the safety of a quiet space, I am beginning to understand why such risks are taken, and I believe that sitting practice is just as dangerous and ultimately more rewarding.

While it may be just an escape from life for some people, jumping out of an airplane seems to hold the potential to make one feel fully alive, to instill appreciation for one's life, build self-confidence, experience completely the present moment, taste personal freedom, and make one grateful for the little things. If you've ever risked danger, then you understand. If you tend always to play it safe, then it's time to flirt a little with danger so that you can truly experience freedom. But there's no need to jump out of a plane. You can experience that, and more, in the quiet of your own home. And after that, you will experience it everywhere you take yourself.

It is not easy to be alone with yourself in relative quiet. No music playing, no busy work in front of you, no distraction. Just you, your mind, your body, your breath. This takes as much courage as jumping out of a plane. The thought of it might even stir up more fear than the thought of jumping. Know that this fear is normal. Know that it is only fear. Know that with practice this fear will subside. And by facing this fear, and yourself, you will build up your confidence and learn to face anything that the world presents to you. You will learn not only to be with yourself but to be in each moment, with each breath that you take. And in each breath that you take you will taste ultimate freedom. You will be free of your fear. You will be free of the grip of attachments. Free to be yourself and to express your inner truth.

I once heard a story of an experienced parachuter that illustrates the danger of not being fully awake to the moment. The person in this story had jumped from planes hundreds, maybe thousands, of times. One day, a typical jumping day, this person reached for the ring that would open his chute. That day, the ring wasn't there. The person panicked and kept grasping for it. When he was scraped off the ground, it was discovered not only that he had clawed his way through his suit to his skin but that his chute was in perfect working order. It seems that jumping out of planes had become so mechanical for this person that he was not fully with himself. For some reason, on this day he used the wrong hand to try to open his chute. And because he was not fully present and was working on automatic pilot, it did not occur to him that he could be wrong. So he panicked, and he fell to an unexpected death.

For most of us in our daily lives, even if we take risks and don't hide from danger, the consequences of inattention are usually not so severe. But how many times have you missed something because you weren't paying attention, something someone said, did, or asked? Do you ever walk into things or people because you are off someplace else, separated from your body? Not paying attention to where you are can actually be more dangerous than what we usually consider a big risk. Because in inattention you are a prisoner of your own mind. And in mindfulness—in an alert, wakeful state—you are free to choose your own path. While you might stumble and fall, you will be able to see the cause of the misstep and know that it is all part of the plan, that you are not a victim of whim.

So, face your dangerous self, go to your *Quiet Corner* with your fear, learn to face it, and conquer it with your breath. Then walk through your life open and ready for anything. Taste the sweet fruit of freedom.

Sometimes, our precious brain can turn out to be our own worst enemy. Our ability to reason is something to be grateful for, but sometimes this ability can overwhelm us and interfere with our spiritual progress. We can find reasons to support any position that we hold, and if asked, we could come up with as many reasons to support an opposing position. We can talk ourselves into and out of anything. We can rationalize even our worst behavior. And we think we can think our way through anything.

And yet, no matter how hard we think, no matter how reasonable the arguments our minds present to us, we are often consumed with doubt. This doubt produces obstacles that impede our forward movement. We allow it to interfere with and determine our way. And it keeps us from trusting our inner voice. Until we are free of doubt, we cannot reach an ultimate state of devotion to ourselves, our lives, our freedom. So, in the stillness of your *Quiet Corner,* begin to observe the workings of your mind. Become familiar with how it lures you by paying attention to your breathing and becoming your mind's witness. Learn to disobey your mind in your *Quiet Corner* so that you can carry this irreverence to the rest of your life.

Most of us grew up learning to obey the rules. We did not want to suffer the consequences of not behaving, so we went along. Unfortunately, our creative thinking suffered as a result. We were not encouraged to think for ourselves. So we got in line, followed the person in front of us, and over the years squashed many of our unique intuitive impulses. Some people act in rebellion to societal demands by intentionally breaking some rules, thwarting the system as much as possible, or not conforming one hundred percent. Some pick up an addiction to drugs or alcohol, which helps them to buck the rules and reach back into themselves to preserve their uniqueness. But all of these behaviors are ultimately self-destructive. So we must first learn to obey the rules without losing ourselves and then learn to disobey the rules and make up our own whenever possible. Complete anarchy is not necessarily the route to ultimate freedom, but anarchy within the structure of conformity is. Setting up a regular routine and structure for sitting still and breathing is the first step in learning how to do this.

The next time you're sitting still, notice how your mind will try to distract you. Become aware that these mind distractions ("I really should be. . . . I wonder what . . .") are nothing but your inability to concentrate. When you have trouble concentrating, your mind rushes in to save you by creating distractions that you believe are real and need immediate attention. So you use them to escape from yourself and then blame your disquietude on something outside you, not taking responsibility even for your own moods. But if you continue to sit still, allowing your mind to do what it does but also allowing yourself to simply disobey its bidding, calmness will follow. You will free yourself from the tyranny of your thoughts. Your thoughts will then just be thoughts, separate from the real you. And you will then be free to hear your inner voice, which is not connected to your brain. Your inner voice rises up and informs you about you, about your true nature and your deep, spiritual truth.

So you can be grateful for your active and curious mind, but you don't need to be controlled by it. You can learn to be its master by spending time in your *Quiet Corner,* concentrating on your breath, and disobeying your mind. You will gain a calmness of mind and a freedom of spirit that you once thought were meant only for a select few. Serenity is available to all of us if we desire it badly enough and take the simple steps that will guarantee it. So you can get what you want when you know what you want. From desire, to being still, to breathing, to serenity.

DO YOURSELF A FAVOR

For one week, spend at least fifteen minutes each day sitting still and concentrating on your breath in your *Quiet Corner*. Keep track in your *Quiet Corner* notebook of your moods, your state of mind—how angry, happy, irritable, or calm you are throughout the week.

Then, for one week spend no time sitting still in your *Quiet Corner*, but continue to document your moods in your notebook. Then compare the beginning of the first week with the beginning of the second. Compare the midweek days of both weeks and the end of both weeks.

Write about what you discovered. Is there a big difference one week to the next? Is your mind finding reasons to justify certain feelings or behaviors? Is your mind telling you that there were many factors that made a difference other than just sitting still?

Try this same experiment for two more weeks. And then again for two more weeks. Do you notice a pattern? What is it? Are the weeks when you spend time in your *Quiet Corner* more balanced and serene? Don't try to figure out why, just accept it as such and keep doing it. Have faith that it works, since you just spent six weeks proving it. Now do yourself a favor and just keep doing it. No more need to keep testing it and denying yourself. Go to your *Quiet Corner*, be there when you're there, and you'll be more available for the rest of your life.

BREAK A RULE

Finding the time to spend in your *Quiet Corner*, write in your notebook, do all the suggested exercises, and also continue to show up for the rest of your life is not always easy. But you can probably, usually, squeak out a little time here and there for sitting still, alone, concentrating on your breathing. You might still feel like your life is moving one thousand miles per hour. Though your mind has slowed down some, you might begin to dream of capturing more time to spend on yourself and your *Quiet Corner* activities. If so, then it's time to be a little naughty and break a rule. This you can do (and maybe should do) even if you can always find plenty of time for yourself. It's simple. Take a mental health day. If you work, take one of your sick days. If you work at home, take a day in the middle of the week and put aside your usual activities. Turn off your phone, hire a babysitter, call the day your own.

Since, unfortunately, our employers have not yet caught up with us and recognized that our mental health is as important as, and closely connected to, our physical health, we simply have to break their rule of only allowing time off to take care of our physical health. There's no need to fabricate a story, simply let it be known that you are ailing and need to take care of yourself. Don't wait until you get sick. Taking time for yourself is preventive medicine. It will keep you mentally and physically healthy. So break the rule in the name of health. And spend a day in the middle of the week concentrating on yourself. Read a book, ride a horse, go to a matinee. Savor every precious second. And begin and end each day with some quiet time sitting still and breathing. You will benefit. Your loved ones will benefit. Your employer will benefit. All for breaking a little rule. The time spent will solidify your *Quiet Corner* practice and confirm to you that you are on the right path.

⦿ PAIN

Surely you know at this point in your life that pain is unavoidable and seems to be a common ingredient in everyone's life. It is all around us, all forms and manner of pain. Yet we spend so much time and energy trying to avoid pain in the pursuit of happiness. What if you were told that pain is not a bad thing? That pain is actually good for you? And that pain is what animates your life, what makes you human? That it can actually make you happy? More than likely, you would probably laugh, ignore such information, and consider it quite crazy. But take a few minutes to consider the possible truth in these statements. Turn off your learned response and open your mind to a little crazy thinking. Just for a few moments. And then decide whether you want to return to your ingrained way of thinking. Decide whether there's room to consider another view.

When I first started doing zazen (sitting meditation) in a Buddhist monastery, I wanted to learn how to stop (or at least slow down) the emotional pain that I was in at the time. I wanted my brain to stop yammering at me. I wanted to gain some peace of mind and internal serenity. Although I was skeptical and didn't believe anything could help me, I was desperate enough to give meditation a chance. So I did what I was told in the hope that it would work. And I got more, much more, than I bargained for.

I sat with the monks and students at the monastery in a meditation hall for forty-five minutes at a time. They were fairly strict and didn't allow much movement during the sitting periods. They told us to count our breaths and not to move. They also told us that trying to move away from any physical pain that we might experience would probably only intensify the pain. I listened, and I sat. I sat with much physical pain, I moved and squirmed, and at moments I hated it. But I did it again, because even though I was in a lot of physical pain, I was so concentrated on it that the other pains I had brought with me paled in comparison. I left that first weekend a little lighter, a little calmer, a little mystified about what actually had happened. I kept doing it despite the pain and eventually learned that all I needed to do to relieve the pain was to accept it. Once you embrace pain, rather than resist it, it tends to dissipate.

A year or so after I started sitting, I did an intensive weekend called a *sesshin*, where we sit all day in forty-five-minute periods broken up by ten minutes of walking meditation. My legs fell asleep, my knees ached, my back hurt, and I wanted to leave many times throughout each day. But I stayed, and I kept trying to bring my attention back to my breath and away from my pain. It worked now and then, but the pain usually persisted. Every time I would move, thinking that I just needed to be in a different position or that a slight adjustment would relieve the intensity of the pain, the pain only got worse. I kept thinking ahead to the end of the weekend, to how many hours, minutes, periods of sitting were left. In my mind I kept leaving where I was and looking forward to the relief I would feel at the end of the weekend. Finally, I just gave up fighting and reconciled myself to the pain. During one period of sitting, I thought to myself, "Okay, just accept the pain. It's only for thirty more minutes. You've come this far. Thirty minutes isn't forever. Just allow that you'll be in this pain, since fighting it isn't working." So I relaxed into the pain, accepted it in my body, and knew it wouldn't be forever. It was only pain now, in this moment. I turned back to my breathing. A few minutes later, my mind became distracted again. Not by pain, but by the lack of it. For the first time all weekend I was free of physical pain. It occurred to me at that moment that the pain was gone because I had accepted it and I wasn't thinking about when it would all be over. How marvelous, I thought. Then my brain moved forward in time and I started thinking about what it would be like to be in that pain-free state for the rest of the sit, for the rest of the day. Suddenly, the pain was back. And I immediately knew that it was because I had moved away from the present moment, because I was trying with my brain to control things. I laughed, relaxed again, and returned to my breathing practice. I was never completely free of pain for the rest of that day, but I learned a huge lesson. And I continue to learn the same thing again and again and again.

Pain can remind us that we're not living in the moment. It can be one of our greatest teachers. The physical pain in sitting can teach you how to honor, accept, and conquer all your other pain. Emotional pain can also be good for you—it can bring you to seek a spiritual practice. Each time you encounter a new pain and think it will last forever, that you've come to the end of the world as you know it, remember that you can learn something new and deeply valuable each time you walk through the pain. Trust that many gifts in life come after much pain. As you start to appreciate this, you will learn to welcome pain without going in search of it. You will learn that pain can invigorate your life and build your character.

So, consider that good things can be bad for you and bad things can be good. Get used to looking at the world upside down. Whenever you have a strong, firmly entrenched position, know that you are probably headed for trouble and some pain. The more flexible and less rigid you are, the less pain you will suffer. There is a big difference between pain and suffering—pain is inevitable, suffering is not. We cause our own suffering when we resist the pain in our lives. Embrace the pain and avoid suffering. Don't run from your pain, and don't chase after joy. As long as you are in the moment with whatever the moment holds for you, pain or joy, you are where you're supposed to be. Unless you embrace the pain, you cannot know the joy that always, inevitably, follows.

PERFECT TEACHERS

Reflect back on the big, painful, traumatic experiences of your life. Write about them. About how they were caused, how you felt, how you handled each one. Then write about what having been through those experiences has meant for you and means for you today. What, if anything, did you learn? If you haven't been aware of the lesson of each painful experience, can you see what that might be as you look back on it now? Write about what each experience still means to you. Write about how each experience has shaped your character and contributed to how you now view the world. Can you see any benefits? What are they? Write about them.

Now write about the positive influences in your life. Your grammar school teacher. Your high school football coach. Your piano teacher. The corner candy store proprietor. Your first theater performance or competition.

Now write about your most difficult or stressful experiences and relationships. Your grammar school teacher. Your high school football coach. Your piano teacher. The corner candy store proprietor. Your first theater performance or competition.

Can you see how you learned something valuable from each experience, not just the "good" ones? Can you take this new knowledge and use it in your life today and know that everything and everybody that you encounter—good or bad, painful or pleasurable—has the potential to teach you something? Can you open your arms and heart and mind to fully accept whatever life presents to you, moment to moment? Without judgment? Without fear? Without expectations?

This may not be possible every moment, under every circumstance, but it can be a goal, it can be something to try for. You will not be perfect every time. And you need to know that even not being perfect is being perfect. That is where you are, in this moment. Therefore it is perfect. Therefore you are perfect. So breathe and be in each moment with you as you are. Perfect.

By now you've learned many ways to bring yourself back to the moment and to keep yourself there. You've also experienced many benefits of continuing this practice. One more way to do this is by moving your body in a very concentrated manner. If you are having a lot of physical difficulty sitting still (pain is fine, but there is no need to torture yourself), you might try walking instead. You can also break up your sitting practice with walking practice. It will stretch your body and your mind in a different way.

If you have a space outdoors where you won't be bothered by traffic, then go outdoors. If not, inside will do just as well. Start by walking very slowly to create a rhythm in your body. Pay attention to your breath just as you do when sitting still. Then pay attention to your gait. As you raise and lower one foot, be aware that you are raising and lowering one foot. As you raise and lower the opposite foot, bring your attention there. If you do this indoors, remove your shoes so that you can really feel your feet making contact with the floor. As you place each foot down, be aware of your heel as it touches the floor, then be aware of the ball of your foot, then your toes. Vary this normal way of stepping by first placing the ball of your foot down, followed by your heel. This may feel a little awkward at first because it's not our normal way of walking, but it will help you to concentrate your attention on your feet. Continue slowly, concentrating on your steps and your breath. Loosely clasp your hands over your navel or behind your back. If this is a strain or not comfortable, then let your arms float at your sides. Send your gaze out in front of you about three feet, and softly focus on the space just above the ground. As you establish a rhythm, you may pick up speed, but don't walk too fast. Keep your pace snail slow if you prefer. Since you will be moving, you will need to be aware of what's around you, so choose a spot with little interference. Or walk with the members of your *Quiet Corner* group, assigning someone the lead position to guide the rest of you; focus on the feet of the person in front of you. As she steps left, you step left. As she steps right, you step right. Try not to look around too much. If your attention is on your breath, you will be aware of your surroundings. So relax, walk, and concentrate on your breath. This is a terrific way to put yourself in the present moment. And you can do this (or a variation of this) anyplace. During your coffee break at work, use the fire stairs, where traffic will be limited. Or close the door of your office and slowly circle your desk. Employ it on a shopping trip to the mall, especially if you find yourself frenetically racing around. Just slow yourself down, and put your attention on your feet as they move one at a time. You'll find that even just ten or twenty paces will settle you down. And remember, this is not about spacing out and walking like a zombie. It's about concentrating on your feet and how they move your body. Five, ten, fifteen minutes. Any and all time is beneficial. One step at a time. One moment at a time. Meditation in motion. A delightful alternative.

10

Practicing What You've Learned

I DON'T KNOW—MAYBE YOU'RE RIGHT—WHAT DO YOU THINK?

Probably the three most difficult words for any one of us to say are "I don't know." Many of us grew up thinking that before we even open our mouths we'd best know what we're talking about. Or what? We'd look stupid or unprepared or uninformed? We'd be embarrassed? We'd be taken advantage of in our not knowing? And so, even if we didn't know, we'd pretend to know, and argue our way through things, needing to be right. Our honor, our pride, our reputation—all at stake. On the average, for someone who has trouble speaking these three words, it takes years of practice—including sitting still, talking to others, writing about self-awareness, moving our body—to begin to feel comfortable admitting not knowing.

Then, once we are able to say "I don't know" and actually feel the freedom that these three small words give us, it takes a few more years of practice before we can truly listen to what someone else has to say on the subject and admit, "Maybe you're right." Because, even though we may not know, especially since we don't know, we think it means that no one else knows either.

Again, our pride at work, doing its job. If we don't know, then no one knows. And if they think they know it's only because they can't say "I don't know." So again we have to beat down our pride, listen to the wisdom of others and admit to them and ourselves that they might be right. This is not easy. It takes time. But, oh, what a glorious feeling it brings to say these words and mean them.

Many more years of practice is necessary before we willingly and eagerly ask, "What do you think?" Prior to this, our seeking out others is usually about what we have to say. And this is very important, because without it we'd never get to this next important stage. So continue to seek the counsel of others and at some point when you're ready, when you've practiced enough, you will notice how easily you ask their opinion. No longer are you attached to your need to be right, your need to know it all. No longer does your pride hold you back from acknowledging the knowledge of others. No longer do you fear what others might suggest to you. In fact, you encourage such input. You have become firm in your self and are no longer so easily swayed by what others might say. Yet you listen well and use much of what you hear readily and with confidence.

Sit still. Talk to others. Move your body. Write things down. Sit with the pain. Don't think. Just breathe.

Sometimes these suggestions may all seem so rigid, strict, so inflexible. But remember, they are only suggestions. And while some of them may be difficult to carry out, they are meant to help you. They are meant to be the ingredients for setting up a framework, a structure for you to use to tap into your inner truth. Once the structure is established, there is freedom and immense flexibility within and around it. You can create your own pattern around the frame of your practice and make it uniquely yours. Once you have a solid base you can swing from the rafters, you can send in a storm, you can shake it madly, and it won't crumble and fall. It will flex with everything you throw at it. And this flexibility will then make its impression on you. And you will gain confidence in yourself and learn to accept with equanimity whatever life serves to you. You will not try to make things or people other than what they are. You will accept a blissful state of being when it arrives. Then you will accept in its place, when it's time, a more subdued state of being, perhaps even a melancholy state. Bliss or sadness— either will be okay with you.

You will become this flexible in your life simply by being inflexible in your practice. By not compromising, by being adamant about reserving some time each day for sitting still and breathing, you will gain a flexible mind beyond compare. By talking to others even when you don't want to, admitting out loud your imperfect human qualities, you will become a human in touch with your inner truth. By writing down your thoughts, your feelings, your deepest secrets, you will open up your pure intention and free a space inside from which will grow love and understanding of yourself and others. And by moving your body, even when lethargy wants to keep you in one place, you will stir up a breeze, clear your mind, and be ready for all that awaits you.

So ask yourself, is it worth being so inflexible with these things just to be flexible in all else? Is ultimate internal freedom worth living with a structure so rigid? Is this structure really so rigid? What is it in me that resists so rigidly? On which side does this rigidity exist? Ask yourself these questions. Write down your answers. Am I flexible? Do I want to be? What does this mean to me? Where is my inflexibility? What am I hanging on to? Can I let go?

When you are truly flexible, you will go to your practice like a moth to light, like a bee to honey. And your flexible mind will create a flexible you. You'll sit in your suit of flexible breath and nothing will surprise you, everything will be filled with wonder. And you will be centered in you, swaying in the breeze, laughing in its beauty, certain of your place in your world.

You might have noticed that when your head is full of noise and you're being tossed and turned around by its energy, or when you dwell in the past or live in your imagination in some future perfect state, time passes so quickly that you hardly notice where it has gone. You wake up one day and wonder why you are where you are and how you got there. What happened to those dreams, those plans, those great ideas? What happened to your life?

Everyone has more than likely experienced some element of this. Perhaps only the most evolved and enlightened beings exist entirely in the moment and are aware of how each moment passes and where the time has gone. For the rest of us, this state is but a goal, and if we are able to achieve this a good percentage of the time then we are on the road to enlightenment. And being on this road, being conscious of our journey is the first step. As we heighten our awareness and begin to accept where we are on this road, then we can use this newborn consciousness to move ourselves along this road, to continue to practice to place ourselves in the moment, and to become more aware of where the time goes and how we've used it, each moment.

Once you begin to hear and trust your deep insights and impulses, it is important to begin to take some actions, however small, to manifest them in your life. When doubt no longer has a stranglehold on you, you can listen without fear, hear where your inner self is guiding you, and take some actions to get there. If you hear the messages that are the truth of you but continue to wait for something to happen, nothing will happen. But if you begin to take some responsibility for your own life and take some actions toward recovering it, miracles will happen. Time will take care of time, and you will not wonder where it all went. You will be in your life and responsible for it.

Living in New York City I have met a lot of aspiring actors. This is where many of them come to be discovered, to get a break, to "make it." They're a dime a dozen, the odds being against making it. I've witnessed many people succumbing to the pain of rejection, which is much of what the grueling road to success in this field is about. Many take it personally and drop out quickly; others stay the course and continue to dream of success, waiting tables and waiting for the big break, their self-esteem eroding with each new rejection. It takes a lot of courage to forge ahead in this very difficult arena.

My friend Sarah has been an inspiration to me as she makes her way as an actress. She has worked very hard on herself and on her career. Over time, I have seen her slowly learn to trust her inner voice, make decisions, and take actions toward achieving her goals and becoming herself. A few years ago, she took a big risk by quitting a rather secure money-making job to pursue her acting career more seriously. She is very talented and was initially very lucky in landing some commercial work that helped pay the bills. Her dream was to become a "legitimate" rather than a commercial actress, but she took any work that came along. At least she was acting. But her inner dream never went away. She struggled to find a manager, an agent, some theater work—to keep the dream alive. Recently she decided that she needed to spend some time in Los Angeles if her real acting career was ever going to happen. I've heard many people talk of going to L.A. Sarah talked, but she also took some action. She began to save money. She took whatever work she could get, acting and not acting, to save money. She contacted some old friends in L.A. and knew she'd have some support when she got there and a place to stay for a while. She decided six months in advance when she should be there. She talked to people about it. She investigated subletting her apartment in New York. She made inquiries about the cost of flying there and having a car at her disposal once there. One day at a time, one small action at a time, she moved herself forward toward L.A.

She was rather terrified yet extremely excited about pursuing her dream. But she neither sat in the fear nor lived in the fantasy. She took concrete actions over the course of six months to realize this dream, never knowing for sure if she'd ever get to L.A. Well, Sarah did get there, and she knows how she did it. She knows where the time went—into planning and dealing with all that came up for her around the planning. She is indeed a brave soul. She was not firmly planted in every single moment of her life over the six months it took to go from plan to execution, but she tried and often succeeded in keeping herself there. She had no idea what L.A. would present to her, but she is way ahead of people who are still dreaming of the chance to be there.

TAKING ACTION

Go back to your life dreams and choose one that appeals most strongly to you in this moment. Or think about one small current desire that is knocking around in your brain wanting expression.

Write a list of what you think you have to do or what you think has to happen for this dream or desire to manifest. Then separate this into two lists—one list of the things you have some control over (List A), one list of the things you don't (List B).

Now, choose the smallest and easiest thing on List A and think of one action you could take toward achieving that thing. Write a letter, make a phone call, purchase something, make a date with someone. Whatever. Then, during the next week, take that action. Don't think of your ultimate dream or what this action might accomplish or how it might move you forward. Don't think about anything that concerns this dream except taking the one small action you've selected.

Then, once you've taken this first action, review List A again. Has taking the first action changed anything? If so, rewrite this list. If not, choose the second easiest thing, and decide to do it before another week passes.

Continue in this manner until you've exhausted List A. What has happened to your dream? Are you closer to it? Has it changed any? Write about it. Sit with it. Breathe it into your belly. Continue to take action and let your dreams come true. For they will. If you participate in the process.

The most important new habit that you will develop as you move along the *Quiet Corner* path is the habit of continually bringing yourself back to the present moment and keeping yourself there. So, as you go through your day, identify old habits that prevent you from practicing this, and slowly work your way toward letting them go. One at a time. It probably will take some time, but you can replace them with new habits, the ones you've learned here. Identify the old ones, name the new ones, and replace the old with the new.

To experience what your life would feel like if you were always in the moment, dedicate one day to mindfulness practice. When you take your shower in the morning, just take your shower. If you normally use this time to be someplace else, remind yourself that you cannot be anyplace else, that you are in the shower now washing your feet, now washing your hair. You can also take your shower in the middle of the day or at night or not at all, to further displace your usual practice. When you eat breakfast, just eat breakfast. Don't read the paper, don't watch TV, don't listen to the news. Just eat breakfast. If you are in the habit of having the TV or radio always on in the background, or if you spend time watching and listening, turn it all off. Let it go for the day. Continue in this manner as you proceed through your day, being mindful, staying with yourself in each moment. This is not an easy thing to do. But you will learn what always being in the moment feels like, and this will inform you in subsequent times when you are not firmly planted in the now. You will become aware much sooner and be able to spend more of your time mindfully. Schedule a day like this once a month if you can. Call it "My day of mindful practice." It is good to do this alone or with others who are committed to the same path, and in as much silence as possible, to gain the full benefits.

Once you establish this first new habit, all the others you need will flow from it. And all your old "bad" habits will roll away and eventually disappear entirely. And if one comes back to visit you, the hyperawareness that you have been cultivating will detect it immediately and your newfound desire for simplicity and serenity will not welcome it. But do not resist it. Let it come, let it try to assert itself, then watch it go. The new life that you are creating will have no room for it.

Old habits can sometimes have a life of their own. So again, be patient (another new habit that you're developing), and time and devotion to your new way of approaching life will take care of you.

Webster's defines habit as "an acquired pattern of behavior that has become almost involuntary as a result of frequent repetition." There have been many suggestions here that at first seem difficult, almost impossible—like sitting still, alone and in silence, concentrating only on your breath. And at first it is difficult. But with repeated attempts, even this most difficult practice can become a habit. Listening, reaching out, putting things on the shelf, turning them over, sharing yourself, taking action, taking risks. These are some of the suggestions that with repetition and practice will become new habits in your life, replacing the old ones. So, if some of the practices suggested here are not yet easy for you, don't despair. With time and repetition they will get easier and will someday become your second nature. You will wonder how you ever lived without them. You will look back at your old habits and have trouble imagining that they were once yours. And the new habits need never go away. They will deepen and grow and fulfill you in ways that you cannot yet imagine. So, edge out the old, work on the new, and keep practicing.

NEW, DESIRED, AND ELUSIVE HABITS

By now, if you've been following along and taking the suggestions you've identified some old habits, you've made some progress with chipping away at them, and you've begun to establish some new habits. Write a list of new habits that you're working on integrating into your everyday life. Write a list of habits that you haven't yet tackled but would like to have in your life. Write a list of habits that you are having trouble with, those that seem to be eluding you. So you'll have three lists:

1. New habits
2. Desired new habits
3. Elusive new habits

With the first list, write about how each new habit appears in your life and what actions you might need to take to further seal it as a habit.

NEW HABIT	CURRENT PRESENCE	ACTION NEEDED
Sitting quietly, concentrating on breath	Seem to find time to do this only two times a week	Schedule time every other day and work toward doing it every day

With the second list, write about one small action you can begin to take to include each desired new habit into your life.

DESIRED NEW HABIT	ACTION NEEDED
Sitting quietly, concentrating on breath	Schedule ten minutes, two times a week, to practice this

With the third list, do the same thing.

NEW HABIT	CURRENT PRESENT	ACTION NEEDED
Sitting quietly, concentrating on breath	Am able to do this only every so often when some other planned activity is canceled at the last minute	Schedule ten minutes, two times a week

Write your lists, work on your new habits, change your life.

Be in the moment, don't project into the future. Stay where you are, since you can't be anyplace else. With all this insistence on staying in the now, you might begin to wonder how you can make plans or in any way prepare for the future. But trying to be in our future before it arrives is very different from planning for the future. The biggest difference between planning and projecting is attitude.

Imagine two friends who have planned a vacation together to Europe. They are both excited about the trip, and it will be the first time abroad for both of them. Chris and Pat live on opposite sides of the airport, so they make arrangements to meet there at the gate. Chris checks the flight time, calculates how long it will take to get to the airport, leaving plenty of time for unexpected traffic problems, and makes plans to leave the house three hours before departure time. The morning is then spent leisurely packing, looking over the maps and books that were purchased for the trip, making phone calls, saying goodbye to friends. Pat, on the other hand, races around like a lunatic, worries about missing the flight, does a last-minute load of laundry, packs and unpacks and packs again. Pat is always late, common knowledge among Pat's friends. And true to form, Pat races around the morning of departure worried about the flight, thinking about missing it, wondering if there would be a later flight if the first is missed. Pat forgets to call ahead for a taxi and is still not ready when it shows up thirty minutes later than it should have. Pat makes it to the airport with only ten minutes to spare but realizes just after boarding that many things have been forgotten—an extra pair of shoes, something to read, the French-English dictionary.

The differences between Chris's and Pat's approaches are clear. Chris planned to catch the scheduled flight and made appropriate arrangements. This made Chris free to put aside all thought of the flight and concentrate on the immediate tasks at hand. Chris was able to be in every moment prior to stepping onto the plane. Pat, however, so worried about missing the flight and projecting negatively into the future, was not in the now. Pat's mind was on the plane, so Pat could not concentrate on packing and planning and arranging a ride to the airport. Hence, Pat was late, things were forgotten, and a state of anxiety was created. While Pat sat in anxiety and stress, Chris sat in relative calm and excited anticipation of what lay ahead for them on the other side of the ocean.

Setting goals in your life and planning for the future does not have to mean taking yourself out of the present. You can comfortably plan future events without leaving the now. It is only when you leap ahead with expectation that things have the potential to go awry. Joyful anticipation, however, is not only okay but a bonus of conscious planning.

So, set goals in your life, make plans, take actions, and then let go and be available for whatever the moment presents to you. This will leave you available for the future moments and all the gifts that they hold for you. Be secure in the knowledge that you have done all that you can do right in this moment to manifest the future plan. And if you have no expectations, the future will unfold as it will, containing whatever you've prepared for; and it will give back to you as much as, and often more than, you've put into it.

Think about the future and plan for it. Just try not to be in it before it gets to you.

No matter how well or how far in advance we plan, we cannot control the outcomes of our plans. Sometimes these plans take us in a direction that we could not conceive of when we made them. Sometimes things work out better than we planned; sometimes they work out worse. When they work out badly, we let ourselves be disappointed. By now, of course, we know that this is because we have expectations; we might have avoided the disappointment if we had anticipated rather than expected the results.

Review some of the goals you've set for yourself over the past five years, and then look at where they are in your life today. Write down the goal, the actions you took to achieve it, and its outcome. Just write this list without judgment. Try not to get bogged down in the quicksand of "I've failed again" if you haven't achieved many of your goals. And if you've achieved every goal you set for yourself, congratulations. For now, let's just look at them.

GOAL	ACTIONS TAKEN	OUTCOME

If you think you haven't set any goals for yourself, then look at the things you have achieved and how you got there. Work backwards. Perhaps you did set goals for yourself but never articulated them as such.

ACHIEVEMENT	ACTIONS TAKEN	IDEA THAT SPURRED ACTION

Now write a list of some things you'd like to accomplish over the next month, the next year, the next five years. Write down one small action you can take to get you closer to each goal, and assign a deadline to accomplishing each task.

	GOAL	FIRST SMALL ACTION TO BE TAKEN	DEADLINE
NEXT MONTH			
NEXT YEAR			
NEXT FIVE YEARS			

Be flexible, be determined, and be willing to let go of any or all of it at any time. Don't hold on too tightly. Don't be too demanding of yourself. Once you write about a goal, a dream, a desire, and get it out of your head onto paper, allow that it will probably change. Give it some space to breathe, to change, to become a gift to you. Monitor your goals, take the actions necessary, but allow them a life of their own—with you the recipient of their gifts. Once you write them down, sit with them, breathe with them, and listen to what your inner voice has to say about them. Keep changing them. Keep taking action. Keep listening. Then, one breath at a time, your life will take shape and become the life you were meant to live.

⊚ WE'LL SEE

We cannot know the future. When I was a little girl, my mother was fond of saying "We'll see" anytime I asked about what might happen tomorrow or the next day or next year. I hated hearing it; I was sure she was holding out on me. Maybe I as a child couldn't see very far, but certainly she as an adult could. As time went on, I was able to accept that maybe some adults couldn't see the future. But I still grew up hoping that I'd be an exception.

Instead, I learned that not knowing what is coming next can make us very happy. Not knowing creates excitement about the future, yet it grounds us in today. We can then anticipate our future with relish. If we write about it and sit with it, we can usually get around to hearing "We'll see, we'll just see." Then we can move back into our current life and let the future unfold as it will.

Remember, though, that some things are predictable. If we don't change our habits and allow unpredictability a wide berth, we will be trapped in a small, stifling life. If we continue to do what we've always done, we'll continue to get what we've always gotten. So change is the imperative here—and an open mind, an open heart. And we must be careful not to fall into the insanity of doing the same things over and over again and then expecting different results. Expectation is not change; it does not change things. Change changes things. It changes you, it changes your life. So don't try to know the future, and don't manipulate the present, thinking you can determine the future. Just breathe, allow time time, and tell yourself, "We'll see. We'll just see."

PUT EARS IN YOUR BELLY

The next time you retreat to your *Quiet Corner* to sit and concentrate on your breath, try the following exercise. Do it each time you're in a state of wanting to know the future. Take your time here. Spend at least fifteen minutes on this exercise.

Once you've settled yourself and are sitting still following your breath, imagine that you have ears in your belly at the end of your breath. Breathe and listen. Breathe and listen with ears deep in your belly. Then just breathe and lose your ears, the ones on your head. Then breathe some more and lose the ones in your belly. Continue to breathe and listen without ears. Just breathe, just listen, no ears.

After this session, write about it. What did you go into the session with? What did you hear with ears? What did you hear without ears? What changed for you during this session?

Repeat this exercise often. Listen with ears. Listen without ears. Can you hear it? Can you know it? Keep breathing. Keep listening. You'll see.

BOOK IV

A Life
Fully Lived

11

A Dynamic
Inner Life

GROWING PAINS

Take yourself back to when you were a teenager. Remember how you felt? Remember the strain your body was under as it grew into its adult form? If you can't remember your own growing pains, do you have or know teenagers that you can observe, to appreciate the growing pains? Have you ever suffered a bodily injury that caused much discomfort as it healed? If you haven't suffered any of the aches and pains of life—physical, mental, or emotional—then you've been quite fortunate. And maybe you won't feel any growing pains as you move along the *Quiet Corner* path either. But most of us feel a great deal as we grow and change, and some of these feelings will not be particularly pleasant to experience. But know that they are normal and natural to the process of change and internal exploration.

When you are uncomfortable, in some psychic pain or emotionally distraught, trust that these pains are necessary, even important, to your spiritual growth. Welcome them when they come, because if you do you might only have to go through the pain once. Many of our *Quiet Corner* growing pains—once we confront them, deal with them, let them run their course, and then let them go—will not return. Some will return with less intensity until we process all that needs processing. And some will continue to haunt us, ever reminding us of our big lessons in life and of our human nature.

You may experience long periods during the *Quiet Corner* process when it feels like nothing is working—you are hearing nothing, feeling nothing, going nowhere. This could mean one of three things: (1) You've reached nirvana and have nothing more to learn, so relax and enjoy it. (2) You are sitting in the calm before the storm, so relax and enjoy it while it lasts. (3) You're cheating and not digging deep enough, so go back a few steps and dig in again. And be patient. Patience itself can produce growing pains. Sitting, waiting, watching, listening. Calmly. Without intervention. You might want to look at the degree of patience that you express in your life. Whether you are experiencing severe growing pains or sitting in a valley of calm, there is ample opportunity to look at your level of tolerance.

If you have seriously been working on yourself and taking the suggestions here, you can't help but move forward. Although at times this forward movement may cause some pain, rejoice, if you can, in this pain, for it most likely signals progress. It is a message that you are waking up, that your interior life is curious and alive, and that you are ready for the next thing. Keep in mind that you are healing and learning new things about yourself. And nothing lasts forever.

DON'T GIVE UP BEFORE THE MIRACLE

We all reach a point in this process when we want to give up, throw in the towel, yell uncle. We can easily get into overwhelm mode with all the internal dynamism, the growing pains. And if we slack off at all on our breathing practice, this overwhelm mode can hit us like a ton of bricks. We might want to go running the other way. A few simple words of caution—don't give up before the miracle. If you ride the wave of discontent, you will be rewarded. Hang in there—joy awaits you.

Can you think of one thing that you abandoned in your life because it got too hard, life got in the way, or someone else influenced your decision? Write about this. Write about your feelings then, your feelings now. Do you have any regrets? If so, can you put this thing back in your life in some way? Chances are you won't be able to pick it up exactly as you dropped it, but be imaginative and think of something to replace it. How does it make you feel to even imagine this thing in your life? Write about that. And if it pleases you, include it in your life again. You won't be sorry.

Can you think of one thing in your life that got difficult for you and that you wanted to abandon, but didn't? (This could be a job, a relationship, a craft, a hobby, an exercise program.) Something you are grateful to have in your life? Write about this. What were the difficulties? Why were you ready to walk away? Why did you stay with it? What makes you grateful to have it in your life today? Did going through the difficulties contribute to its preciousness? Is it more of a miracle as a result? Write about all this.

Use these writings as inspiration anytime you hit a wall in the *Quiet Corner* process. Learn from these that giving up is not an option, that goodness will reveal itself. Be patient. Breathe. And then bask in the miracles of your life.

It has been said that making art is a process of discovery. A brilliant work of art does not appear in final form, magically, all at once. The conception might be fully formed in the artist's imagination, but the art itself takes time to create, and during the creative process little discoveries are made and factored into the final form. Nothing worthwhile, nothing of interest, nothing with depth and character gets created or formed instantly and completely. A process of creation is necessary.

Just so with our lives. Life is a process of discovery. We cannot think ourselves or will ourselves into something other. We can only shift into something other, move into new and unexplored territory, slowly, one step at a time. But this doesn't have to mean that every moment must be planned, every second accounted for and scheduled. In fact, this approach can be stifling, as you learn to create your life, as you wake up your inner voice and learn to express your true self.

Your new life is created by allowing your inner self to come forward and out. It is an inside job. Rather than look outside yourself and try to fill yourself up with what you see to make yourself whole, you learn that you need to look inward and create yourself from what you find there. You need to enter into the flow of your life. If you fill your life too full, it will not flow easily, it will crash up against itself, against all those things you've put in your way. So it's crucial to leave some empty space in your life. Leave room for the unexpected. Leave space in which you can explore and discover new things that will add spark to the life you are creating. Engage in some spontaneous behavior. Leaving space in your life allows for this. Remaining bogged down in compulsive behavior—which comes from your head, your ego, your fear—will keep you stuck and bored. Moving into spontaneity—following impulses that stem from your heart, your belly, your breath—will make your life more alive, more intuitive, more creative, more fun.

If you've come this far on the *Quiet Corner* path and you've been taking the time to sit still and breathe, your daily priorities will shift. You will find time for yourself, for spontaneity, for healthy spiritual reflection. You will shuffle the deck of cards that is your life and come up with a winning hand every day that you commit yourself to the *Quiet Corner* practice. And you will begin to allow space for yourself in which to grow and gain serenity.

So think of yourself and your life as a blank canvas on which you are applying the paint that will form the color of your life as a work of art. Or imagine that you are a huge block of precious wood or marble and your *Quiet Corner* practices are the sculpting tools that will form the eventual you. Imagine a ball of unformed clay, a bolt of fabric, or an untuned piano. You have all the necessary equipment right in front of you, at your disposal. There is no need to go hunting for more. It is not necessary to waste another moment. It is time to get started. Just begin, and you will make discoveries as you go. Dig deep, trust your instincts. Take some chances, breathe and dream, and learn to listen. Find your center, your creative self. And then unlock it, open it up to the world, and create your own dance, your own symphony of your own life. Let yourself go. Be spontaneous. Be courageous. Be alive. You will know what to do. Take the chance and let your inner world show you the way. It's an exciting way to travel. So go in, open up, and let go. The trip of your life is in progress and carrying you back to you. Bon voyage!

DARE TO FAIL

Spontaneity can be difficult to entertain, especially for those of us who like to control things or who like to think that we control things. For those of us who have something scheduled every minute of every day, even the idea of spontaneity can seem like a luxury. But we have to give up control. We have to find the time in our busy schedules to relax and allow our spontaneous natures a bit of freedom. And, like almost everything else, we need to practice it until we can get good enough at it not to have to think about doing it, until it becomes second nature. As usual, we will not be perfect. But if we don't dare to fail, we will never gain.

So, though this may sound paradoxical at first, schedule some time to just simply do nothing. Plan to spend an hour or so the first week doing nothing. Your first reaction to this suggestion might be, "But I don't have an hour a week to spare," or "Doing nothing is such a waste of time." Hear this voice and then put it aside. Tell yourself that one hour is not so much time. One hour out of 168 can be found someplace. And if you've done the suggested exercises up to this point, your mind will be calmer, your anxiety will be much reduced, and your schedule will be more manageable. You will no longer be bringing as much work home on weekends, you will recruit help in caring for the kids, you will replace procrastination with mindful action, you will honor yourself and your needs. So for one hour a week, do not do chores, do not keep busy, do not fill the time with your usual activities. Daydream. Let your imagination run wild. See what happens. When some thought comes up of what you might like to do, check in with yourself and make sure it's not just to fill time because you're uncomfortable doing nothing. If you're not sure what spontaneous feels like, you will get to know it after a while.

Be spontaneous. See what happens. As you begin to cultivate spontaneity during this hour that you regularly set aside for it, begin to experiment with it in the rest of your life. If you feel a spontaneous impulse to do or say something, then do or say it. Dare to fail. Listen to this inner you and go for it. Feel the freedom it brings you. Bask in it. Delight in it. Keep doing it.

You'll get the hang of it, sooner or later. And your life will eventually be seamless. Spontaneity will be so integrated into your behavior that there will be no jarring movement to or from it. It will just be another interesting facet of your new, complex, and wonderfully free existence.

⑥ EXERCISE YOUR RIGHT BRAIN

Life is a mystery. We cannot begin to understand everything, but if we give up the compulsion to try, then a fuller understanding comes. And it doesn't come from our abilities to analyze and think deeply—it comes from other parts of us. Our intuition, our gut, our senses. Someplace other than our left brain. Our left brain, which we couldn't live in society without, helps us to make sense of things. It contains our center for rational thought, and we are trained from a very early age how to use this necessary body part. But so many of us become off-center, lopsided, from using our left brain almost exclusively. We're not taught or encouraged to use our right brain, which contains our creative centers, our imaginations, our intuition, the spice that contributes greatly to our individuality, our creative differences and uniqueness. Think of a left-handed tennis player and how from using his left arm every day and almost exclusively it becomes larger, stronger, more developed than the right arm. That is how most of our brains are—the left side is more developed.

Much of what we're doing with our *Quiet Corner* practice is trying to balance this load, to shift it from our left brain and use our other faculties more. And although much of what we begin to grasp through our *Quiet Corner* practice may not come exclusively from our right-brain (it may come from some place other than our brain entirely), it is important to exercise our right brain to achieve some sort of balance. We need to stop thinking so much. We need to stop trying to figure it all out. We need to let go of that and trust that understanding will come even, and especially, if we're not working from our left brain. Once you let go of thought, as you've probably already experienced from your *Quiet Corner* sitting practice, you can go elsewhere, you can go deeper inside yourself, exploring new, fertile territory that exists outside your left brain.

Anytime you encounter resistance throughout this process (and you probably will) more than likely it is your left brain talking. Whenever you notice yourself thinking too much, your left brain is responsible. So move to the other side. Look at something beautiful. Draw a picture. Bake a cake. Challenge yourself creatively. Don't think about what you're doing. Don't judge. Don't criticize. Those are all left-brain activities. Let go. Dream. Imagine. Dance. Turn your world upside down. Look at your world upside down. A quick and effective way to do this is simply to bend over and look through your legs and back up at the world. Outside in full view of trees and sky is a great place to feel the immediate impact of this. The view is still beautiful and colorful, but it's different. It's upside down. Breathe it in. What do you see from that angle that you don't see when you're upright? Pay attention to it. Notice the details. Do this with the rest of your life. Look at everything upside down, literally or figuratively, and notice the difference. Do this especially when you feel stuck and when you're centered in left-brain activity. Look elsewhere inside you. There's a lot more going on. Take advantage of the energy your left brain creates and move it elsewhere. Wake up your right brain with it. Nudge your heart and gut with it. Stir things up. Allow your left brain to watch as the rest of you starts to play.

Like everything else, it takes practice to get good at this. Even now, right this moment, just think about everything inside you waking up. Send your breath, right this moment, to your heart, your belly, your toes. Can't you just feel it? Their potential is awesome. And you are the coach. So go for it. Train that right brain. Bench the left. And you'll be prepared for everything that comes your way—a well-balanced, well-trained, flexible mind, heart, and spirit. Who would want anything else?

DREAMS

When you begin to quiet your left brain and allow other internal activity to take place, your inner voice becomes louder, clearer. Your inner life becomes more dynamic. Even your dreams are wilder and freer. If you've been writing down your night dreams, you might want to look at how they've changed over time. These written dreams are a great source for some right-brain activity.

Start by drawing pictures of some of your dreams. It doesn't have to make sense and doesn't have to be a literal interpretation or rendering of your dream. The drawing that is sparked by one of your dreams may take off in a new and different direction once you begin. It may have nothing to do with the dream. That's okay. Just go with it. Go wherever it takes you. Don't let your left brain tell you, "But you're supposed to be drawing your dream." Let your right brain take you wherever it wants to take you. Do this exercise often. It's great right-brain practice. And, as you know, practice is practice. And practice creates balance. And balance keeps us centered. And the center is where we want to be. Practice, balance, center. Use this as your right-brain mantra. It will keep you on course.

⑥ FEELINGS

There is danger in waking up internally, which is probably why so many of us stopped doing it long ago. We get in touch with our feelings. And even though you're beginning to learn to take risks, this fear in dealing with feelings as they come up can paralyze us.

Once we wake up all our senses, our feelings come alive. Unfortunately, confronting our feelings can seem like a big deal. Especially in the beginning. Especially when the feelings that get stirred up are old and have been buried and festering for a long time. Especially when these feelings make us feel like one big, raw, exposed nerve. Our insides get that weird, tingling, somewhat painful, somewhat refreshing sensation similar to what it feels like when a leg or arm has fallen asleep and then starts to come back to life. But try to remember. These are only feelings. They won't kill you. They are not the facts. The pain will eventually stop, and you will be fully awake and able to move with no stubborn, buried feelings weighing you down.

One thing that often happens when this process of waking feelings is in full swing is that you take most everything that happens to and around you very personally. You will be so sensitized and vulnerable that you won't be able to avoid this. But remember, everything that happens to and around you is not always about you. In fact, you can bet that it isn't about you at all. It simply feels as though it is. So, allow the feeling, let it run its course, and don't be swayed by your self-centered ego fantasies.

At some point, you will not only be in touch with your feelings, you'll be able to express them. And as you learn more about your inner voice you will know the appropriate expression of your feelings. You will continue to feel hurt, sad, lonely, happy, joyous, glad, angry, blue, or ecstatic. And you will be able to identify the feeling, express it, and move on. Sit in it as long as necessary, but try not to wallow in it. Admit it, let it be, whatever it is, and don't be tossed away by it.

ACKNOWLEDGE YOUR FEELINGS

When your feelings are in full bloom and seem to be getting the best of you, it is important to remind yourself that you are simply having feelings. These feelings will change. Remember that you are much more than feelings.

I am not suggesting that you try to get past these feelings. You must acknowledge them and have them. But there is no need to get tossed around or blown away by them. This tends to happen when we allow our feelings to enter our left brain and we start *thinking* about them. Therefore, it is a good idea to ground yourself, especially if you feel an oncoming storm or if you begin to think too much about how you're feeling. Your usual breathing practice is, of course, ideal. Concentrating on your breath rather than on how you feel will change how you feel.

But sometimes we just can't sit still; we need an interim activity. So if you're feeling restless and overwhelmed with feelings, begin to ground yourself by closing your eyes and taking three deep, three-part breaths. Then write about what you're feeling. Try not to get swept away. Just write about your feelings and what they seem to be doing to you. Then turn to a fresh page and write a description of yourself. Start by describing how you look—not how you feel about how you look, but how you look. Use a mirror or picture of yourself to see yourself better. Then describe your personality as others might see you. Then go on and fill in other pertinent details about your work, your family, your interests. Write in the third person. Draw a portrait of yourself in words. And then draw another picture of yourself using paint or crayons or watercolors. Be playful here. And be flexible.

If during this process you want to go off on tangents and write about or draw something else, then go there. Don't constrain yourself. There are no rules here except your own.

When you've come to the end of this exercise, try again to sit and concentrate on your breath. Any easier than before? Then write about your feelings again. Has anything changed? Write about that. If your feelings haven't changed, how about your acceptance of them?

Like everything else, we cannot really control our feelings. And we now know that ignoring them is not an alternative, since that is most likely what put us here in the first place. So the best course of action is just to accept them, try to understand them, and let them go. Like everything else. Simple, but not easy.

When we are not bogged down in thought, overwhelmed with feelings, or paralyzed with fear or some other pain, we are free and open to hearing the truth about ourselves and, if we're lucky, some bigger, deeper truths. Getting rid of all the voices in us that don't belong and then sitting still so that we might hear what we are all about, what belongs to us, as you've surely discovered by now, is a process that takes time and patience. And practice. And failure. And humor. And courage. But the rewards are worth the effort. If you've done any of the suggested exercises up to this point you've already reaped some benefits. Calmness of mind perhaps? Or greater awareness of others? An easier acceptance of that which you cannot control? These are all big things and definitely yours if you continue on the *Quiet Corner* path.

We also gain smaller things along the way. Often, the impact of these small things can be more powerful and richer than the big ones. The small things build on one another. Like gaining a fresh appreciation for your morning cup of coffee because you've been taking the time to sit and savor it. Or beginning to see how your partner's habit of always being late is not an affront to you, she does it with everyone, it is her quirk, you can do nothing about it.

At first glance, these things appear small, and we convince ourselves that no progress is being made. But if you can replace *small* with *big* or use neither adjective to describe these things, then they are what they are, and they are new and different. Accept that and they become "bigger" and they come "faster" and more frequently. And then together they combine to become calmness of mind, acceptance, awareness, serenity.

Just so with insight. This is a big word and implies big things. Inner awakenings that unlock the mysteries of the universe. Deep understanding of the how and the why of things. The meaning of our lives. While such truths are absolutely available to you, they may not come all at once. They may not appear as a flash of light illuminating your ignorance; they may not be epiphanous and singular, coming up from you fully formed and wondrous. Though this *may* happen to you, it is a good idea not to expect it but to appreciate the smaller, seemingly less profound miracles that rise up. These may come suddenly and from nowhere. They can range from finally making sense of why your aunt decided to tell you that Santa Claus doesn't exist, to deciding to give away your old computer, to realizing that your best friend truly is your best friend. Do not throw these away. Do not think they are not important. Know that they are your insights, personal to your life, and unique to you. While at first you might consider them mundane and not "spiritual," remind yourself that that voice is an old one and one not to mind. Trust that these mundane insights are important, and that they, like many other things, build on each other and combine to form something bigger. Perhaps together they will solve for you the mystery of the universe. Maybe they will provide clues to all human nature. For sure, they will complete the picture of who you are and how you fit into the world.

These insights come to all of us, and we need to be alert to them. Sitting quietly and concentrating on your breath is the practice that prepares you for hearing your inner voice, your insights. But it is not only during this quiet time that insights make themselves known to us. In fact, many inner thoughts, feelings, and realizations rise up when we're not sitting still. But chances are they won't rise to the surface if we don't sit. This practice helps to quiet our minds so that we can hear our inner truth even when we're not exactly quiet. So, for instance, in the middle of a business meeting, out of the blue, in an instant, it might occur to you how to solve the problem you had been grappling with the night before. Or during a movie that completely holds your attention you might think of just the right thing to say to your boss, without really even thinking about it. Small things? Yes and no. Insights? Definitely. So prepare yourself, trust that inner voice wherever and whenever it speaks to you, and all will be revealed. (Well, maybe not all. Even Einstein admitted that he couldn't understand it all.)

So allow the insights. Allow the mystery to remain. And find the joy and wisdom in the small things.

Let's get back for a moment to the subject of prayer and the power it has in our lives. Much of what we've been doing throughout this *Quiet Corner* process is a form of prayer. If we consider that prayer is communing with God, or with whatever we choose to call God, and that sitting and breathing is a form of listening for the answers, then indeed we have been including prayer in this process. Each time we acknowledge that we aren't doing any of this alone and then write or talk to someone else about what is going on inside us, we are offering up a prayer. Each time we become aware that we are not in the moment, pick up our purpose tool to bring ourselves back, and then add a dose of gratitude to the mix, we are offering up a prayer. Each time we ask for help, each time we admit not knowing, each time we earnestly wish to be shown the way—we are offering up a prayer.

The next time you use your purpose tool or write in your *Quiet Corner* notebook, consider it a form of praying. This acknowledgment will add a new dimension to each activity and perhaps help you to appreciate the significance of all that you are doing here. When you approach your life and everything that you do on the *Quiet Corner* path honestly and with integrity, then your whole life becomes a prayer, devoted to your higher being.

Formalizing and ritualizing prayer will appeal to many of you. Decide for yourself how you want to do this. Reserve a time first thing in the morning or last thing at night to pray. Kneel at the back of your favorite church at lunchtime. Use the ride to work each day to commune with your higher power. Do something—and here is the key—*every day,* to include prayer in your life. If you look closely, you probably already do this. Putting a name to it will simply make it more sacred and meaningful.

CREATE A PRAYER

If you don't already have a formal prayer practice, you might want to create one. And remember, this doesn't have to be "religious" if you don't want it to be. It simply has to involve some ideal that is higher than you and your ego. So begin by selecting a prayer or two to recite each day. If you know no prayers or can't find any to suit you, then write your own. You may want to do this anyway so that your prayers are tailored to your life and your unique circumstances. Here are some elements to include in your prayers:

- An appeal for help
- An admission of your own powerlessness
- Humility
- Thoughts of others

Can you think of other things to include in your prayers? Write a list and use that as a starting point.

It is a good idea to begin by praying for others. Pray that your loved ones will be blessed with what they need. Pray that those you still harbor resentments against will get more than what they want. Pray that those who have lost their way will once again find it. Admit and then pray for all that is out of your control. Pray for acceptance, courage, and wisdom.

Be yourself when you pray. No one else is watching. You are on your own in the company of your higher power. Keep your judge, critic, and ego at bay. Keep your prayers in your heart and mind throughout the day so that they are easily accessible if you run up against a wall. Take them out and use them in the crowded elevator or subway car. Clear everything else away, breathe, and pray. The moment will change. And prayer will be your guide.

LIVING EVERY MOMENT
FULLY ENGAGED

You cannot think your way through all problems and circumstances. Little by little, you begin to accept this as you travel further down the *Quiet Corner* path. You begin to recognize how your past was ruled by your thoughts. And as you become acquainted with all your other internal workings, you see how thinking is just a small part of all that contributes to your awareness and understanding of things. You begin to acknowledge and nurture your other faculties and begin to achieve an emotional and spiritual balance. It is very exciting and life affirming that first moment when the mental click happens and you know, deep inside yourself, that something has changed, that you are different, that you are more fully and wholly yourself. This is a magnificent feeling and yet can quickly move from the extraordinary to the ordinary if we don't continually remind ourselves from whence we came. Being human, we can so easily take our transformation for granted and believe that this is how it always was and always will be. Be careful about this. Keep your practice going. Be diligent and humble, and you'll avoid this trap and its inevitable downslide to old behaviors. Continue to use your *Quiet Corner* tools so that you keep moving forward. More and greater awarenesses are always up ahead. Don't take all the credit for your progress—give some to your higher power, to other people, to the mysterious workings of the universe. Continue to practice acceptance, turning it over, breathing, sitting still, and, of course, listening.

Listen when you're sitting. Listen when you're walking. Listen when you're doing the dishes. Listen at work, when you're with the kids, as you're falling asleep or in love, while riding a bike, or reading the newspaper. Listen while you eat, as you argue with a friend.

Listening doesn't mean stepping back and observing. It means moving closer, being engaged in your life without clinging. It means not chasing thoughts but letting the thoughts come to you. It means not chasing anything, letting it all come to you—awareness, acceptance, insight, understanding, serenity, peace of mind. It means paying attention first to your breath and then to whatever your breath carries back to you. Listen, and you shall receive. Listen, and you will hear. Listen, and you will know. Listening will open you up. Listening will give you the world. It is the key that will unlock the universe for you. And you will then swim in its mystery and revel in its glory.

12

The Power
of Silence

YOU ARE DOING THIS ALONE

You've asked for help, you've shared your secrets, you've opened your heart to others. You've admitted the union you have with all humanity, and you've relied on your higher power to see you through each day. All these connections to "other" are crucial and necessary if you are to make spiritual progress along the *Quiet Corner* path. But, only you can take the necessary actions to reach out, to make those connections, to pray, to sit quietly and breathe. No one else can do these things for you. It is up to you. You are in charge of your life. And in this way you are alone. That first step off the diving board is yours to take; no one will push you. That giant leap off the cliff is your decision; no one is chasing you. You are responsible for putting yourself on the *Quiet Corner* path. Otherwise, it wouldn't work. Being solely responsible for our chosen path, we have no one to blame when the going gets rough, only lessons to learn.

Sometimes when sitting alone in silence, the realization hits us that we are indeed profoundly alone. This can be quite terrifying and perhaps even existentially unnerving. This feeling that comes up, and it inevitably will, is one that we'd all like to escape.

And for just this reason many of us avoid sitting alone in silence. We're happy to do everything else, but this we just cannot do. We'd rather live in denial than confront ourselves alone. But this is one step that we cannot skip if we wish to be free.

Even though we may know intellectually and deep in our hearts that we are alone, in many ways we create distance from this truth. Keeping busy and constantly surrounding ourselves with noise are just two ways of dodging it. When we place ourselves in silence, we cannot hide from it. It drives itself home to us with intense power. We have no choice but to face it. And as with any fear, once faced, it loses its power over us. The power of silence is greater than anything that enters it. It can absorb and soften and cradle all that it is offered. Approach it as your partner, your friend. Be alone *with* the silence rather than *in* the silence. Let its power support, not threaten, you. You alone can ignite its power, and it is your choice whether it is to be menacing or comforting. It is powerful, but you have power over it. So use it to face yourself and your aloneness. Don't shrink from it or from yourself.

Only when you establish a relationship with silence and are able to sit comfortably with it does your inner life become dynamic and open to the miracles of the universe. In silence, we nurture our souls, learn about ourselves and others, hear our inner voice, face our deepest fears, welcome our profoundest joys, and practice all that we need to know to get alone in our nonsilent lives. Here we begin to take baby steps toward developing a powerful practice of prayer and meditation. Here we learn that anything, absolutely anything, is possible. We begin to envision for ourselves a life beyond our wildest dreams, where we acknowledge to ourselves that such a life is ours almost for the asking.

Silence. Go to it as you would a teacher. Trust it as you would your dearest friend. Allow it into your life to embrace you, comfort you, teach you, and guide you. For it is capable of all this and more. Silence. Think of it as an energy force, dynamic and powerful. Color it with benevolence, and you will seek it out gladly. It will never disappoint as long as you let it be in charge. Give over the reins of your life to it and let it lead you. If you are having trouble acknowledging a God or a higher power, use silence instead. Once you adopt it, enter it, and let it perform its job, it will expand around you and contain all that you need to bring peace to your world and, especially, your mind.

If you are struggling with a thorny emotional issue, bring it to the silence until a solution appears. And it will. Whenever you think you have an answer to a problem that has plagued you, bring it to the silence before you take an action. It will either support your solution or caution you to wait for a richer one. Before you do anything that affects your interpersonal relationships, play it out in the silence, alone, with the silence as your mentor. Check your motives. Run through the various scenarios, testing your commitment. Be sure that you know that only you can be responsible for your thoughts, your feelings, your actions, no matter how sincere your intent. If you feel that it's time to let a dear friend know that you know that your behavior in the past was hurtful to them, do not expect them to be grateful and forgiving right away. Be content simply to make your amends, take responsibility for your actions, and give the other person the freedom to react in whatever way is necessary for them to process this. Or if you are ready to forgive someone their abusive behavior toward you, don't expect them to change simply because you've forgiven them. Do it simply to be free of the burden of resentment and animosity. If you take these things to the silence before you act, you will know what to do and when to do it. The silence will coach you. The silence will ease your doubt. The silence will always be there.

Sometimes, especially if we have hyperactive imaginations, we might hear things in the silence that surprise us, even shock us. And though at first glance they are outrageous, we believe them, we accept them as truth, because they make themselves known in the silence that we've learned to trust. But not everything that comes to us in the silence is truth. Some of it is diversionary and delusional, nothing serious as long as we don't take it seriously. And there is only one way to know the truth. Keep going back to the silence. If it's diversionary and delusional, it will fade and reveal its true colors sooner or later. If you are in a relationship that is emotionally troubling and you bring it and your pain to the silence, you might at first hear in it that your partner is intent on harming you and is to blame for all that is not right with the relationship. This makes you feel better, it exonerates you, and your next move seems clear. But before you do or say anything, take it once again to the silence. Chances are, a second exposure to silence will reshape your problem somewhat. You might begin to see that all is not his fault, he is not such a bad person, and you haven't been an angel. A third time will alter your vision even more. By the time it all settles down, you will arrive at your truth—what you need, what you have, what you can do. Sometimes we get so attached to our delusions that we let our minds convince us that they are real. In such cases, they hang around a long while, supporting our theory that they are real. You might keep insisting that he is the devil and you are the angel. But that is only your mind conjuring against you. So be careful. Sit in the silence long enough and you will know. Let the doubt in. Listen to yourself. Trust yourself. Let go. If it's real and the truth and an honest answer, it will continue to appear, it will gain strength. You will know without doubt that it is real and part of your inner truth.

Keep going to the silence. Carry it around with you. It is only one breath away. Close your eyes. Take a deep breath. Anywhere. Anytime. Let the silence envelop you. Let it bolster you. Let it renew and guide you. You are alone in it, but it is your company. Use it and see how it readily and immediately connects you to all that surrounds you. We are all in it together, this soup of silence, and it is strong enough to hold us all. So if you test it, use it, swim in it, we all benefit. We all feel the waves of your movement.

Before we begin retreating into the silence, many of us have the idea that silence is without sound, absent of noise, pure and dreamily quiet. And since we are usually surrounded by sound and quite at home in it, the idea of quiet might be anathema. So we avoid it for as long as we can because even the idea of the absence of sound frightens us on some level. Then when we finally decide that we must learn to sit still in the quiet, we cannot believe how not quiet this quiet is. We expect to find perfect stillness. When we slow down and begin to concentrate on our breathing, we become hyperaware of all the sounds surrounding us. And these at first become such a distraction that we blame them for our inability to concentrate. So we go in search of a truly quiet place, thinking that we cannot do this breathing practice until we find the quiet. So we search and search and eventually discover that unless we seal ourselves off from everything, no place is perfectly quiet. This is the beginning of learning how to find the quiet in a not-so-quiet world. This is the beginning of allowing sound to be sound.

Once we accept the external noises and allow that silence can include them, we notice again how loud silence can be. We notice the birds singing, the heat rising, the traffic humming, and we accommodate these sounds into our silence. But then we encounter the noise of our brains working, and we get distracted once again and become frustrated that silence is so noisy. Sometimes we retreat into the noise of music or crowds or a movie to drown out the noise of silence. And then we figure out that this is only avoidance and that life and the truth are in that noisy silence. We must return there again and again to face our internal noise, to learn how to let the externals be what they are, and to delve deeper into the noise of silence to get to the pure essence of the quiet in our minds.

So when you retreat to your *Quiet Corner,* be aware that the quiet you expect may not be there to greet you. Once you slow down, become still, and concentrate on your breathing, you will hear as you've never heard before. You will distinguish each sound as it visits you, and this awareness will offer you solace. Accept these sounds as sounds, and don't allow them to disturb your inner peace. This will teach you to accept your internal noises and to treat them as you do the external ones. Let them be; you have no control over them. Just breathe and move away with your breath. The sounds will not change, but the way you hear them will change. You will still be sitting in loud silence, but you will be in touch with a quiet place deep inside that will overwhelm the noise and center you in peace.

13

Being in
the World

TAKING RESPONSIBILITY FOR
YOUR LIFE

Whenever we emerge from our *Quiet Corners*, where we've sat in
the silence and worked through our issues in our hearts and
minds, we have to face the world and practice there what we've
practiced alone. The challenges of life sometimes come at us at a
pace that seems quicker than we think we're prepared for. But if
we've done our work and if we continue to pray, meditate, and
retreat to our *Quiet Corners*, we will be able to handle anything
that life serves up to us. As long as we remember that we are
responsible for *our* actions, *our* thoughts, *our* behavior, that we
have no control over others, and that our job is to take that
responsibility for ourselves, then everything will fall into place.
Everything will be manageable.

We will be most challenged in our relationships with other
people. This is where we can test how well we've learned the
Quiet Corner principles, where everything that we face in life will
get played out. Here we can learn to take responsibility for our
actions.

Consider your work. The talent and skills that you bring to

work are important, but your success can best be measured in your relationships with your co-workers and superiors. If you cannot communicate well (or if your ego interferes with your productivity or you can't get along with your boss), then it won't really matter how brilliant you are at your job. But if you carry what you've learned here into the workplace, you will show up with enthusiasm, you will not point your finger, you will communicate your needs without anger. You will share yourself willingly, your good ego will shine, and, best of all, you will gain more enjoyment from each day, from each moment, than ever before. This is taking responsibility for your life at work.

Consider your intimate relationships. You will begin to approach them in strength, knowing clearly who you are and what you need. Rather than placing blame and being ego dependent, you will take responsibility for your half and allow others to express their unique selves without demanding that they conform to your vision. You will reach out to others with love and get love in return. You will loosen your reins of control and move closer to further intimacy. It will be easier for you to let go of your need to be right and let relationships unfold naturally and spontaneously. This is taking responsibility for your life at love.

Consider all your other relationships—with strangers on a crowded subway, with neighbors, with your children's teachers and their friends' parents. With your car mechanic and grocery clerk. With your tennis partner. When you become intimate with yourself and understand and take responsibility for how you present yourself to the world, all encounters with other people will either become more pleasant or be seen as opportunities for growth. You will no longer see yourself as a pawn or victim. You will see your part in every relationship, and you will know how to handle yourself or be open to changing your behavior. This is taking responsibility for your life at home and at play.

So be responsible and take charge of your life. Then turn it and the rest of the world over to your God and others. You will benefit. Others will benefit. Life will then be better than anything you might have imagined. Take your place as assistant director of your life. And then breathe in the freedom and perfect balance of your life.

⑥ CLARITY

One of the rewards of *Quiet Corner* practice that begins to reveal itself from the very beginning and continues to deepen and expand throughout this process is that of emotional balance and clarity. When we take the time to clear our minds, to engage in introspection, to sort things out and talk them through, and to pray and then sit quietly alone focusing on our breath, we can't help but gain perspective, acceptance, and, finally, clarity. We can't help but find internal peace and calmness of mind. We can't help but know that everything happens for a reason and whatever answers we are searching for will be revealed to us in time. And we begin to see that time takes time and we are not necessarily the best judge of when, where, and how. At some point, even this becomes okay with us.

But we are all only human, and our path toward spiritual peace will not run smoothly and gracefully. Rather, we will travel along as though on an upward spiral, dipping backward on every turn before moving upward again. Each time we hit one of these natural dips in the road, we might get confused and feel like no progress is being made. It might occur to us, since it feels like we're slipping backward, that maybe we're doing it all wrong, that something more or different needs to happen. Each time this thought appears, remember that dipping backward is a normal and integral part of the process. Each time you hit a natural dip, know that it is an opportunity for growth. You are not doing anything wrong, it only feels that way. Keep doing your sitting and your breathing, and the feeling will pass; you will be at the next level. Each time you get this feeling that you're doing something wrong, it might mean that you are simply looking for and expecting certain results, that you are trying to control an outcome. So rather than heeding that voice, simply let it have its say and then let it go. Rather than allowing that voice to keep you in your head, simply leave it there and move into your belly. Find your center again. Don't allow the negativity to throw you around. Sit, breathe, go to your center. Sit there for a while. Breathe. Then open up. Open up to see your position on the spiral of life and accept wherever you are. Open up and realize that you are doing it all perfectly right. Open up and know that you are where you are supposed to be and that you have everything you need—nothing more, nothing less.

This self-clarity that you gain from the *Quiet Corner* process will then serve you as you look outward to the world. You will see that everyone in your life is on their own path and that you have no power or control over them. This realization will indeed be a relief, and you will bask in the resulting freedom. As you look outward with your newfound clarity and keener intuition, you will glide through your day easily handling situations that once might have tripped you up and baffled you. Your newly honed awareness and your mindfulness practice will lead you to make the connection between your *Quiet Corner* practice and the new ease with which you deal with your life and the people in it. This realization will then further your commitment to your *Quiet Corner* practice, and your *Quiet Corner* practice will in turn continue to enhance your life and improve your clarity. This will strengthen your resolve to practice more, which will clarify more. And on and on. Spiraling up. Dipping down. It is all important and necessary. It will all bear fruit. And at some point, if you keep up your practice, you will savor its sweetness.

Before we enter onto the *Quiet Corner* path and gain self-aware-ness and clarity, our relationships with others may be troubled. Perhaps we have problems with intimacy that cause us to feel that we can trust no one and so live much of our time alone and isolated. Or maybe we feel that we can never be alone, so we develop an unhealthy need to be so close to people that we find ourselves uncomfortable unless we are merged with someone else. We might use people for our own selfish needs and attempt to control and manipulate their behavior. Or we are so unaware of our own desires that we allow others to define us and dictate our behavior, which creates resentment, animosity, and insecurity. While you may not identify exclusively with any of these scenar-ios, perhaps you can relate to a small measure of each. Once you enter onto the *Quiet Corner* path, all this can and will change. In our relationships with others, we can first identify our own growth and progress along the *Quiet Corner* path. It will take some time, but healthy, loving, intimate relationships are possible. And it all begins with you. Not with them. It begins with you and your willingness to practice unconditional love.

Forgiving others is one important tool that works to open your heart, to let love in, and to express love. At times, this will be your greatest challenge. Forgiving when your heart has been broken is not easy. But if you look closely and if you are honest with yourself, you will usually notice that it is not your heart that prevents you from extending your love and forgiving others. It is almost always your ego that gets in the way of this most healing of gestures.

Remember, harboring anger and resentment in your heart toward someone else because of their behavior toward you hurts no one but yourself. Others may not even be aware of the hurt they caused. Your anger hurts you much more than it hurts them, and besides, hurting them is probably not your honest intention anyway. So realize that forgiveness and love is what you can give to the relationship to begin the healing. Forgive first, and then communicate your hurt if it still feels important. Don't wait for the other person to admit guilt before you forgive. And don't wait until you express your anger before you forgive them, hoping for something from them. You have no control over them. It is not up to them to remove the hurt. Only you can do that, and forgiveness is the way.

"I understand." How comforting these words are. Even when they come from a stranger. No matter what we do or what our intentions are, we all want to be understood. Yet sometimes this need gets in our way and prevents us from expressing love and forgiveness. It closes our heart, as we wait to be understood before we're ready to share ourselves. If we can flip this around in those moments when we are desperate or simply in need of being understood, and instead seek to understand rather than be understood, imagine the repercussions. Your heart would open as you reached out, trying to understand with no self-serving intentions. Your mind would also open to allow differences and to accept the history that defines others as other and separate from you. The hurt in your heart would abate as you became aware of the hurt in the hearts of others. Your own experience with hurt would allow you to express empathy and compassion. Love would boomerang back to you as it moved out toward others. You would allow others to be themselves and not take their idiosyncratic behavior personally. You would see the charm and uniqueness in others and no longer want them to change to suit you.

Another useful tool to use for opening your heart is not placing impossible expectations and demands on others. Once you stop this and start forgiving, all your relationships will improve. You will approach them with detached love and understanding and have no need for them to define you or fill you up. You will experience how giving unconditionally to others benefits you. You will come to know how service to others is the ultimate spiritual act. As long as there are no expectations and no need for recompense, then service to others will become your raison d'être. It will supply meaning to your life, it will bring ecstatic joy, and it will make you humble and loving and available for the love of others.

In a scene in the movie *Marvin's Room*, Diane Keaton's character tells her sister, played by Meryl Streep, how lucky she has been in life. Even though she is herself struggling with a terminal illness and has spent most of her life caring for her aunt and bedridden father, she expresses her joy at having had so much love in her life. Her sister nods and agrees that the father and aunt do love her dearly. But Diane Keaton goes on to say that she meant something else. She meant that she felt lucky to have been able to love them so much. It is a very poignant and almost shocking moment in the movie simply because we are so rarely shown this kind of love. Keaton's character gave her love so unconditionally that she didn't need nor was she looking for love in return. Loving others was more than enough. Loving them enriched her life completely. This kind of love is available to all of us. We just have to find it in ourselves.

Once you stop blaming, start forgiving, and begin doing service, you will be open to this kind of love. You will be living in the stream of goodness and spiritual health. And once you change, others may change. It is even possible for the whole world to change—for politicians to begin caring about people, for parents to put their children first, for teachers to give more to their students. All this begins with you and me and our small worlds. Our spiritual and giving energy will enter the larger pool of human energy and slowly shift the flow toward forgiveness and service. This is possible. Anything is possible. But without even thinking of this bigger benefit, do it anyway. For you, for your spiritual practice, and for the love that it will induce. Love, forgiveness, service. That's all we need.

WRITE A LOVE LETTER

Write about love and what it means to you. Write about the things, people, and situations in your life that you love. Write about how others love you. Write about how you love others.

Write a love letter to yourself. Or more than one. Write the letter you've always wanted to receive from your romantic love interest. Write one to you, from you; from your God; from your mother or father; from your cat; from an imaginary friend or someone you don't know too well.

Write a love letter to someone else. Write a love letter to someone toward whom you are still holding a resentment. Write one to your dog, your boss, your neighbor.

Bring these letters to your *Quiet Corner* sharing group and read them out loud. Listen to others read their letters. Accept the emotions. Accept the tears. Accept the laughter or grief. You will touch something deep inside you. You will all hear and breathe your inner truth, singly and collectively. You will walk away clearer—your heart open, your inner voice singing.

Language can be very powerful. While this may sound simplistic, I think we all forget at times the subtle yet blatant power that words have over us. The language we choose can inspire us, or it can defeat us. It can excite, motivate, hurt, challenge, confuse, or please us. The language we use toward others not only affects others but communicates to them much about ourselves. Language and its delivery lets others know not only how we're feeling about them but also how we're feeling about ourselves. If we are feeling angry or loving toward another, the language we choose will reveal these feelings either directly or often quite indirectly, especially if we are out of touch with our own feelings or if we are attempting to hide them.

Whatever we are feeling about ourselves will be communicated to others through the language we use. If, when we are alone, we indulge in self-criticism and self-judgment, no matter how hard we try to prevent it we will continue to use such self-deprecating language when speaking with others. And of course the reverse is true. If we practice the language of self-love while alone in our *Quiet Corners,* we will speak with love when around others. Whatever self-referential language we use will spill into the rest of our lives and influence the words we use in the company of others. So listen to yourself, listen to others, closely read what you've written in your *Quiet Corner* notebook, and learn to choose your words carefully. They are precious carriers of meaning and can be luscious carriers of love.

We want to aspire to the language of love on the *Quiet Corner* path. Both alone in your *Quiet Corner* and out in the world with others, be aware of the words you choose, become attentive to your language, and practice moving toward loving speech. Both arenas, alone and in company, are ripe for honing your language skills. When alone in your *Quiet Corner,* each time you notice yourself using self-defeating or nonloving language, stop and choose different words. Even if you don't quite mean it yet, begin to use more positive, loving language. And when talking with others, if you can catch yourself before uttering a self-critical or judgmental word, change it to a more loving word, or simply even a neutral one, if loving is too great a reach at that moment. If you don't catch yourself before letting the word or phrase out, then immediately apologize, and rephrase your expression.

Practice, make mistakes, don't be too hard on yourself. You have used language habitually for years. Learning a new language takes time and patience. But you are now beginning to find time for your *Quiet Corner* pursuits, and by doing so your patience is growing. So you will have time and patience. And learning the language of love is well worth spending a lot of both. So listen as others speak and decide how you like to be spoken to. Listen to yourself as you speak to yourself and then to others, and decide which language you prefer.

FLIP YOUR WORLD AROUND

Now that you are practiced in the ritual of *Quiet Corner* journal writing, take a look at the words you use to think with, speak with, write with, and feel with. The language with which you choose to express yourself is one key to understanding who you are and what you want from yourself and others.

Take a moment now to write in your *Quiet Corner* notebook how language influences you. Think of when you fell in love and the words used during that time by you and your partner. What was so special about those words? Or think of your last argument with a loved one or even with a co-worker. Write down the key words that come to mind. Don't edit yourself. How might either of these experiences been different had you chosen different words?

Each time you visit your *Quiet Corner*, pay special attention to the specific language of your thoughts and feelings. Are there recurring themes? What are the words you would use to describe them? Write about that. Look through your notebook and notice your language. What mood do you create with your words? Is it the mood that you intended when you first wrote those words? If not, think about how it is different and write about that. If you succeeded in capturing your mood, write about that now. How does time change things? What new perspective, if any, do you have about yourself? Write about that.

It's usually quite instructive to review our past thoughts and feelings. New and provocative insights into our character are usually gained. Our self-awareness deepens, and our sensitivity and compassion toward others increase. As you begin to notice particular patterns in your language, start flipping things around. The idea here is to try to see yourself, your world, and your habitual ways of thinking and approaching the world in a fresh way. In essence, you want to completely flip your world around. For instance, if you notice that you often express yourself by using the words "If only," try instead to replace that expression with the words "I will." The following is a short list of words with suggested alternatives.

I wish . . .	I plan . . .
I can't . . .	I'll try . . .
I know . . .	I don't know . . .
I don't know . . .	I know . . .

There is, of course, a plethora of such phrases that each of us uses and uses and uses again. What are some of your recurring or even favorite such phrases? You may not even be aware of how often you repeat yourself. This is one reason why keeping a journal can be so instructive. Reread what you've written. Try to detach yourself from it. Pretend you are not the author. What do you hear? What phrases recur, and what would the flip side of those phrases be? Write a list. What benefits can you imagine from this exercise? Write about this.

Continue to practice rewriting the language you choose, and try to become aware of how you use your everyday speech. Ask the people closest to you to help you identify the self-defeating words you use, as you are using them. Try to be open to hearing what they say, and make an attempt to rephrase your words on the spot. Bring this newfound knowledge about yourself into your *Quiet Corner* and sit quietly with it. Try not to judge yourself. Just listen to how your mind constructs things. See the words and let them go. Don't reach out to the words, let them come to you and then let them go. Remember to breathe as you continue to do this, and then write about the experience. Do all this over and over and over again. Establish a rhythm for yourself in this activity, and allow yourself to express your thoughts and feelings, however they need expression. Have some fun with it. Think of it as a verbal adventure into your nonverbal world and an exploration into your deepest, truest self.

⑥ ACT AS IF

As you progress along the *Quiet Corner* path, your approach to life and your attitude toward it will shift. As you learn to lighten up and let go, the heaviness in your heart will go away, and you won't continue to take life so seriously. You will embrace both the laughter and the tears that come your way and know that together they combine to make you human.

Sometimes, no matter how hard we try, no matter how much we know, no matter how strong our desire, we get bogged down in a feeling, a mind state, an obsession. While accepting these states as part of us and then allowing them to run their natural course is the ideal way to process them, sometimes we allow ourselves to wallow, sometimes we like to hang on to our misery, sometimes we need extra help. And sometimes we know we need to move away from certain situations no matter how strong the pull. At such times, we need to act "as if."

If you find yourself stuck in an overly serious mode with gravity pulling you deeper in, act "as if" you are enjoying yourself, having a grand old time stuck in the muck. If you are having trouble forgiving someone and expressing love, act "as if" you love them. Use words of love even if you don't yet mean them. If you are stuck in tomorrow wondering what will happen, act "as if" it doesn't matter, act "as if" today is the most important day of your life—even though you "know" it isn't, even though you "know" you are fooling yourself. Act "as if" you like your boss. Act "as if" your mother-in-law doesn't drive you crazy. Act "as if" you are happy to be alive.

Someday, you will no longer have to act. You will like your boss, your mother-in-law will not drive you crazy, you will be happy to be alive. Just keep acting "as if" until something changes. And change will happen. If we can count on nothing else, we can count on change. Nothing remains as it is forever. It is as it is only in this moment. It changes to another as-it-isness in the next moment. And so on and so on. Accept the as-it-isness of life. And if you can't accept it "as it is," then act "as if."

BE MASTER OF ALL OF
YOUR EVERYTHING

We all face challenges throughout our lives, whether or not we choose to travel along the *Quiet Corner* path. Putting ourselves on this path, however, gives us tools to confront our life's challenges with equanimity. Being on this path, we learn to accept whatever is put in front of us as something that we can learn and grow from. We choose not only to face these challenges but to look deep into ourselves and listen to our inner truth, to hear what makes us tick, and to know what colors our unique outlook.

If you can accept that walking through difficulties and experiencing pain can result in eventual bliss and that continuous bliss might even become boring and useless, then you will indeed enter into boundless and eternal joy, and your heart will be luminous. And no matter what happens—"good" or "bad"—you will live your life in harmony. As you learn to expect nothing, you will engage with your life as never before. You will know your own limits, and you will gain an appreciation of others as your own personal truth becomes crystal clear.

Rather than struggling and forcing your way through each day, you will begin to wear your life like a loose garment. There will be no chafing or unnecessary discomfort from a tight, restricted fit. You will have room in which to grow and change. You will have the freedom to move comfortably and protect yourself from extreme temperatures. And you will adapt to changing circumstances without strain, without worry, without undue suffering.

Have you ever watched a cat chase after its own tail? She delights in the fun of this all-absorbing activity and doesn't express frustration at never catching and holding onto it. This is the approach we should take with our lives—seeing what we want, going after it with all our attention and spirit, delighting in the process, and being open to something new and different that might cross our path.

So step on this path, choose any higher power as your companion, and take hold of the oars as you glide to a fresh shore. And then just keep listening. You will know what to do next. Sit, breathe, and *just listen*. And with love, gratitude, and peaceful serenity, become the master of all of your everything.